Mission Overseas

Mission Overseas

Daring Operations by the Indian Military

Sushant Singh

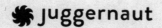

JUGGERNAUT BOOKS
KS House, 118 Shahpur Jat, New Delhi 110049, India

First published by Juggernaut Books 2017

10 9 8 7 6 5 4 3 2

ISBN 9789386228178

Typeset in Adobe Caslon Pro by R. Ajith Kumar, New Delhi

Printed at Manipal Technologies Ltd

To Anukruti and Aviral

Contents

Introduction

On the Indian Defence Minister Manohar Parrikar's first official visit to the Pentagon in December 2015, he was asked if his government would be willing to provide soldiers to fight the Islamic State terrorist group, also known as ISIS or Daesh. Parrikar dodged the question, saying that India only sent its soldiers abroad under the United Nations (UN) flag.

That is the official reason trotted out by Indian ministers, generals and diplomats. Army chiefs have gone on record to say that Indian soldiers couldn't fight along with NATO forces in Afghanistan as it was not a UN mission. It is true that most Indian soldiers who have served abroad have done so under the UN flag. In fact, with more than 180,000 men – and, lately, women – having served as Blue Helmets, India is the biggest contributor of soldiers to UN peacekeeping operations. But as everyone suspects, and knows, the UN flag is a fig leaf of an excuse.

New Delhi hasn't always looked towards the UN headquarters for a go-ahead before sending its troops abroad. Leave aside the 1971 Bangladesh war, there are other instances that are hardly spoken about. In 2001, for instance, the Bharatiya Janata Party (BJP) government came very close to sending an Indian army brigade to Iraq after the then deputy prime minister and home minister, L.K. Advani, and others, promised the Americans the same. At the last moment, Prime Minister Atal Bihari Vajpayee took a contrarian call, saving India the ignominy of being seen as an invader á la Bush's America.

The most famous of India's overseas missions is Operation Pawan, the thirty-month-long operation by the Indian Peace Keeping Force (IPKF) in Sri Lanka against Prabhakaran's Liberation Tigers of Tamil Eelam (LTTE). This was a full-fledged out of area (OOA) operation – as the military calls an overseas mission – in which the Indian army fought on its own in a foreign land for an extended period. Unfortunately, the Sri Lankan operation ended in disaster and, with the IPKF pulling out without achieving its objectives, it became the most powerful argument against future Indian military involvement overseas. The ghost of Operation Pawan hung over the proposals for similar Indian missions in Iraq and Afghanistan and, recently, against ISIS.

The Sri Lankan precedent provided compelling logic

against getting entangled in a full-fledged overseas mission. So while Narendra Modi's government conducted *limited* military operations inside Myanmar in 2015 and Pakistan-Occupied Kashmir in 2016, India did not intervene – its warships and fighter jets did not even stage a symbolic show of strength – when the deposed Maldivian president Mohamed Nasheed was put behind bars after being 'convicted' under anti-terrorism legislation in February 2015. Earlier, in 2012, the democratically elected President Nasheed had looked towards India for help when he was overthrown after a coup by his political opponents. But both the BJP and its predecessor, the United Progressive Alliance (UPA), chose to follow a policy of non-intervention.

In 2012 and 2015 Nasheed had had great expectations of New Delhi, and for valid reasons. In 1988 his uncle Maumoon Abdul Gayoom was the president of the Maldives when a coup was attempted with the help of Sri Lankan rebels. President Gayoom sent an SOS message to many countries, including India, Pakistan, Sri Lanka and the United States. But before anyone else could react, Prime Minister Rajiv Gandhi took the call to send Indian paratroopers to the Maldivian capital of Malé, post-haste.

Code-named Operation Cactus, that mission was sharp, short and successful. It achieved its aim of restoring the civilian government, and more. While the result was perfect, the making of the sausage wasn't that nice. The story behind Operation Cactus has never been fully told. I was fortunate enough to lay my hands on the parachute brigade's official after-action reports and Brigadier Farooq 'Bull' Bulsara's personal memoirs, and interview half a dozen key participants to get the full picture of this emergency mission.

As in all successful military operations, luck played a major part in this one too. Good fortune is especially important if you launch a military strike in a foreign land armed with tourist maps and coffee-table books, and intelligence dating back to the Second World War. But along with luck, the boldness of the military commander, Brigadier Bulsara, and the supporting role played by the then Indian high commissioner in Malé, A.K. Banerjee, contributed to its success. Most important, however, was the willingness of the political leadership to take tough calls decisively, despite limited information. The decision-making was centred in the Prime Minister's Office (PMO), with Ronen Sen playing a major role. But the man who made it possible, according to Sen, was Kuldip Sahdev, then joint secretary in charge of the Maldives in the Ministry of External Affairs (MEA).

It is rather hard to imagine now, but after getting an early-morning call about the coup in Malé, Sahdev first phoned the Indian Air Force (IAF) to ask them to get the aircraft ready. Only then did he call the PMO, and the foreign secretary was informed only after the MEA office opened at 9.30 a.m. There was great clarity in the military and the bureaucracy on India's role and the strategic challenges in the neighbourhood. They knew what the political leadership would decide to do in a scenario like the Maldives coup, a situation today's policy planners can only dream of.

If the media coverage of Operation Cactus was flattering – and rightly so – there was an equal amount of criticism of the IPKF's operations in Sri Lanka. The bevy of Indian and foreign journalists in Colombo started calling the Indian briefings 'Five o'Clock Follies', reminiscent of the moniker given to the infamous US military briefings at Saigon in Vietnam. This was fitting in many ways, particularly because Sri Lanka was indeed India's Vietnam.

In a conflict between irregulars and a professional army, the irregulars are perceived as victorious if they simply survive. The Tamil Tigers were certainly able to survive, and the Indian military's boastful pronouncements at the launch of Operation Pawan that they would finish off the Tigers in a week came back to haunt New Delhi.

There was little domestic support – public or political – for Indian military action in Sri Lanka. The country did not understand why its soldiers were in a foreign country in the first place, and beyond a point it stopped caring. In Tamil Nadu, the only Indian state deeply interested in Sri Lankan politics, there was widespread opposition to military action against the LTTE.

So all of Rajiv Gandhi's political opponents, led by V.P. Singh, promised to bring back the IPKF, and they kept that promise after the National Front government came to power in 1989. But no leader from that coalition, supported by both the BJP and the Left parties, even went to symbolically receive the Indian troops when they landed at Palam airport in Delhi.

Policymakers of that period have two justifications for Operation Pawan. One, they were able to prevent other foreign powers from meddling in India's neighbourhood; and two, India ensured that Sri Lanka did not break up and remained a single country. There is merit in both arguments, even though the price India paid, from the loss of Rajiv Gandhi to the denting of its military reputation, was substantial.

While there is hardly any authoritative material on the Maldives operation, the IPKF's Sri Lanka campaign has been written about extensively – there are books, monographs, memoirs, pamphlets, papers and articles galore. However, there is not much written information about those first days of Operation Pawan, which signalled what an enormous challenge the LTTE was going to pose for the Indian army.

The LTTE had been funded, trained and equipped by India in the years preceding the operation. In Sri Lanka, Prabhakaran and the LTTE were seen as an Indian creation and no one expected them to stand up to New Delhi's diktats. After the LTTE and the IPKF fell out – the IPKF's handing over of LTTE prisoners to the Sri Lankan army was the breaking point in an already deteriorating relationship – the Indian army decided to capture Jaffna, the LTTE headquarters. In a bold operation, they chose to land an infantry company at the Jaffna University grounds at night.

One of the Indian army's elite para commando battalions, 10 Para, was tasked as the vanguard of the heliborne mission. From planning to execution, the operation was an unmitigated disaster. The IAF helicopters ferrying soldiers to Jaffna University were shot at by LTTE fighters positioned on the university buildings, and only thirty-two men of the infantry battalion could land there. They didn't survive for long. The para commandos at the forefront of the operation were trapped by LTTE fighters in a residential neighbourhood near the university. The story of what happened to them over the next thirty-seven hours has never been told before. Tanks were blown up, senior officers leading rescue teams were taken out by rebel snipers, and LTTE fighters kept coming at the Indian soldiers relentlessly, in waves. This episode squelched forever the dismissive talk of the LTTE being 'bloody lungi-walas who can't fight'.

All societies celebrate military victories and slowly forget military disasters. But disasters hold bigger lessons for the future. That's why it is important to study the Jaffna University operation, even though it isn't a pretty picture.

The final overseas mission covered in this book is different from the other two in most aspects. It took place in the year 2000, not in the 1980s. It was not in the neighbourhood, but 10,000 kilometres away, in Africa. It was under the UN umbrella, and it involved operating with other foreign militaries. But it was still, in essence, an Indian military operation. It was launched to rescue 223 Indian soldiers who had been kept under siege by rebels in Sierra Leone for seventy-five days. The commander of the UN force in Sierra Leone was an Indian general, Major General V.K. Jetley. The bulk of the forces used, particularly for the main operation, were Indian. And the final go-ahead for Operation Khukri, as it was christened by the Indians, was given by South Block in New Delhi.

The operation was a military triumph but the events preceding the military engagement were a lesson in politics, intrigue and diplomatic manoeuvring. The Force Commander Jetley had to go to extreme lengths to keep his operational plans secret from other UN officials, fearing leaks and the plans being compromised. He did this for good reason. India was clearly on its own: the Americans and the British had refused to help rescue the captured Indian soldiers; the Nigerians seemed to almost delight in Delhi's discomfort; and the UN Secretary General, Kofi Annan, seemed keen on distancing himself from Operation Khukri. He told Jetley, in response to the Force Commander's request that a military operation be launched to free the Indian soldiers, that *he* should be the one to decide. General Jetley ultimately took the bull by the horns and, with support from the Indian government, pulled off a spectacular success.

Those who argue for the cover of a UN flag and a multinational force for the Indian military to operate overseas need to study Operation Khukri. The constraints imposed by wearing the Blue Helmet – the sensitivities of other countries and the web of politics and allegiances that determine the motivation of other nations' militaries and governments – can make the simplest of tasks complex. Mindful of this lesson, the Indian government had ensured that in the deployment plan to send an Indian brigade to Iraq in 2001, the Indian army would have been put in charge of a separate Kurd-dominated region. It would thus have avoided the problems it faced in Sierra Leone.

As India becomes a greater power, especially in the neighbourhood, that time is not far when the Indian military may have to operate overseas again. Currently it may appear that we lack the political will to send our troops abroad, but that could change rapidly. However, change will be slow in the creation of military capabilities and the right mindset for overseas operations. Once these enabling ingredients have been assembled, our decision-makers will not have to proffer the excuse of a UN mission; if our strategic interests dictate a particular course of action, it will be taken. If the recounting of Operations Cactus, Pawan and Khukri can initiate a discussion on the need for preparing the Indian military for overseas operations, this book would have served its purpose.

Finally, another common feature of these three operations is that their official Indian army histories have not yet been made public. There is no valid reason to keep them under wraps and it is my sincere hope that this book will trigger the government to declassify these details.

Official history or not, these operations are an integral part of independent India's history. They hold salutary lessons for us even today and thus must be read.

Operation Cactus:
Mission Impossible in
the Maldives

On 3 November 1988 in the early hours of the morning, a deadly coup was mounted in the Maldives. The President of the Maldives sent a desperate SOS message to India from his secret underground safe house, prompting Prime Minister Rajiv Gandhi to swiftly come to his aid by launching one of the most daring operations ever by the Indian armed forces. What unfolded was one of India's proudest moments in which a flamboyant brigadier, a bemused ambassador, a daredevil bunch of paratroopers and ace pilots, and an intrepid navy captain came together to do the impossible.

It's been twenty-seven years, but Smita Prakash still remembers the events of 3 November 1988 as if it were yesterday. It was her wedding day. Midway through the jaimala ceremony – the exchange of garlands between the bride and the groom – she noticed that the crowd of guests had begun to thin.

Smita's father, Ram Mohan Rao, was principal information officer in the Prime Minister's Office (PMO). He had been at work till 6.30 p.m., reaching the wedding venue just a short while before the groom, Sanjiv, and his party arrived for the ceremony at 8 p.m. Sanjiv was the India correspondent of NBC News; Smita too was a journalist. So the guests at the wedding included a large number of press.

'I looked around, saw people leaving, and asked Sanjiv, "What's going on?"' Smita recalls.

While the guests thought they were whispering sweet nothings, Sanjiv told Smita that there had been a coup in the Maldives, and that G. Parthasarathy, information adviser and spokesman in the PMO, had walked into the wedding and was rounding up journalists to cover the army operation being launched there. The government didn't want a repeat of what had happened during Operation Blue Star in June 1984. Then, the Indian army had gone to clear terrorists from the holiest shrine of the Sikhs, the Golden Temple at Amritsar, amid a total media blackout. The absence of journalists led to careless rumours flying about, and a tense, charged, highly negative atmosphere around the operation which eventually resulted in the assassination of Prime Minister Indira Gandhi by her Sikh bodyguards.

Partha, as everyone calls G. Parthasarathy, is a retired Indian Foreign Service (IFS) officer who now spends his time on various think tank forums and is a familiar face on television. He remembers that opinions were fiercely divided on whether the media should witness the Maldives operation or not. Prime Minister Rajiv Gandhi eventually took a firm decision at three thirty that afternoon in favour of it. But Partha remembers bypassing the defence secretary, T.N. Seshan – who later became famous as a hardnosed chief election commissioner – and requisitioning an aircraft for the journalists directly from the Indian Air Force (IAF). As Partha got busy managing the complex media arrangements, the prime minister had a special instruction for him. '*Time* is doing a major piece on India's rise as a regional power. Please make sure that Ross Amroe, the *Time* journalist who met me for the story, is on board,' Gandhi told him. Partha called Amroe and asked him to head directly to Kheria airport in Agra, where instructions were given to let him in. He then collected all the journalists, photographers and video cameramen at Smita's wedding – leaving the poor bride and bridegroom without much of a celebration. Smita, now an editor at ANI, still regrets the fact that there was no video recording of her wedding ceremony, till a replacement videographer arrived much later.

'As soon as the ceremony got over, Dad went straight back to work at the PMO,' she recounts.

~

The PMO may have been bustling but most of the action was actually taking place at the office complex in the prime minister's residence at 7 Race Course Road. 7 RCR (as it is commonly called) is not one bungalow but a twelve-acre complex in Lutyens' Delhi, comprising five bungalows. Unlike 10 Downing Street, 7 RCR does not house the prime minister's formal office, but has a small office space for the prime minister's secretarial staff to work out of.

Ronen Sen, an IFS officer who later served as the Indian ambassador to the United States and played a major role in swinging the India–US nuclear deal, was a joint secretary in the PMO for many years. He was seen as one of the prime minister's favourite officials and, unlike his predecessors or successors, had unprecedented access to him.

Under his quiet demeanour, Sen is a man of sharp, astute views and strong opinions, shaped by his experiences in the PMO from the 1960s to the 1990s. As a special assistant to Indira Gandhi's close aide and confidant P.N. Dhar in the PMO from 1969, he had witnessed the 1971 India–Pakistan war and the liberation of Bangladesh and India's first nuclear test in 1974.

'In Rajiv's PMO, barely 15 per cent of my time was spent on foreign policy. I spent much more time on issues which went beyond external affairs – space, atomic energy, security – especially as I was handling the intelligence agencies for the PM,' Sen recalls.

On 3 November 1988, he remembers waking up to an early morning phone call. It was from Kuldip Sahdev, joint secretary (BSM) in the foreign ministry, informing him of the coup in the Maldives. (BSM stood for Burma, Sri Lanka and the Maldives, and Rajiv Gandhi was fond of ribbing Sahdev at conferences that every country under his watch was in trouble.)

Sahdev remembers that assignment as the most challenging and exciting one of his career. With Indian peacekeeping operations in Sri Lanka against the Liberation Tigers of Tamil Eelam (LTTE) in full swing and Aung San Suu Kyi returning to Burma in 1988 and agitating against the military junta, those were indeed turbulent times.

At around 6 a.m. on 3 November, Sahdev was woken up by a call from the acting Indian high commissioner at Malé, who informed him of some shooting taking place in the city.

The predawn silence in Malé, the capital of the Maldives, a remote Indian Ocean archipelago, was broken that day by the sound of machine guns, rockets and grenades. The peaceful country, which didn't even have a proper army, was being attacked by seaborne raiders. They had struck at selected targets including the president's residence and the headquarters of the Maldivian National Security Service (NSS) and taken over key government buildings such as the radio and TV headquarters, and cut off the electricity and water supply in Malé.

Half an hour later Sahdev got another call from the acting high commissioner. This time it was more urgent. He confirmed that Malé was under attack and asked if India should help. His source was Ibrahim Hussein Zaki, then foreign secretary of the Maldives.

The raiders were later identified as Tamil mercenaries from Sri Lanka, belonging to the People's Liberation Organization of Tamil Eelam (PLOTE), headed by Uma Maheshwaran. PLOTE had initially been funded and supported by Indian intelligence agencies as a counterpoise to the LTTE. The group that launched the coup in the Maldives had been funded, recruited, armed and trained by a few disgruntled expatriate Maldivians led by a businessman named Abdullah Luthufi and his associate Sikka Ahmed Ismail Manik. The eighty-strong team of raiders landed at Malé before dawn, using speedboats from a freighter. Several other PLOTE mercenaries, disguised as tourists, had entered the Maldives earlier.

President Gayoom, an Islamic scholar and cricket fanatic, was then fifty. President since 1978, the diminutive, balding figure was widely respected and into his third consecutive term. The Maldives had a form of indirect democracy, where the President was elected by the Majlis (parliament) which in turn was elected through consensus by the people. There was no direct voting or election for the Majlis.

On 3 November President Gayoom was expected to have been in India and the plotters, to whom his travel schedule had been leaked, planned to strike while he was away. The Indian aircraft sent to bring Gayoom to Delhi was mid-air when the trip was cancelled. Rajiv Gandhi had to unexpectedly travel out of Delhi for an election campaign, and he and Gayoom decided it was best to put off the visit for the time being. Undeterred, the ringleaders of the coup decided to go ahead with their plans.

~

The Indian high commissioner to Malé, A.K. Banerjee, had reached Delhi two days before Gayoom's scheduled visit – protocol requires the presence of the envoy whenever a head of state or government visits India. With the visit postponed, Banerjee took a few days' leave to spend time with his family in India. He had been high commissioner to the Maldives for over a year, since 21 July 1987, and knew Gayoom well, even playing cricket with him regularly.

A mild-mannered man, Banerjee is a retired career diplomat who feels that he did not get his due from the government. He was at his father's house at Defence Colony in Delhi on the day and planned to drop in at the MEA at South Block.

'I was comfortably asleep, wrapped in my quilt, when I was woken up by a call at around six thirty on 3 November. The caller was my secretary from the high commission in Malé. He told me that since four thirty that morning, there had been incessant shooting and the gunmen were on the streets. They had attacked the NSS office and killed several people. The Maldivians were retaliating but they were outnumbered and outclassed. The gunmen, apparently Sri Lankan Tamils, were trying to capture the president and overthrow the government. The Maldivians wanted India to help them and asked me to intervene since I was in Delhi,' recounts Banerjee.

Banerjee was stunned by this news. His first thoughts were of concern for his staff in Malé and he asked if the Indian high commission personnel were safe. His secretary reassured him but added ominously, 'Who can give any assurance in these circumstances?'

There was more news. President Gayoom was, according to Banerjee's secretary's source, in a safe house and the request for help had come personally from him. Appeals had also gone out to other neighbouring countries including Malaysia and Pakistan.

Banerjee later found out that his secretary was being briefed by Anbaree Sattar, President Gayoom's chief security officer. Sattar had managed to reach the secretary's house incognito to relay this message to India. President Gayoom trusted Sattar implicitly and, years later, rewarded him by making him minister for defence and later still, high commissioner to India.

Taken aback by the attempted coup, Gayoom had

asked not only India, Sri Lanka, Pakistan and Malaysia but other countries, including the United States and the United Kingdom, and the Commonwealth organization for help. The Sri Lankan government in turn asked India to provide an IAF aircraft so that their soldiers could be airlifted to the Maldives.

Pakistan, according to an Indian official who was privy to the deliberations among the military brass at Rawalpindi, was reluctant to move its troops so far, across the Arabian Sea and the Indian Ocean, with no assured help from India. The Americans would have to move troops from their base in Diego Garcia, and it would take them a couple of days to even reach Malé. The UK and the Commonwealth organization were also not in a position to help promptly.

India, in contrast, was already involved in an overseas military operation in Sri Lanka. Rajiv Gandhi had made it clear to his team of officials that the neighbourhood was India's zone of influence. India, as the largest country in South Asia, had to bear the fallout of conflicts and unrest in its smaller neighbouring countries, and needed to be prepared to play its rightful role in the region.

Against that backdrop, Indian officials were able to swiftly put together a plan of action. As soon as Sahdev got off the call from Malé, he called Air Vice Marshal Denzil Keelor to tell him to ready an IAF team for the

Maldives. Sahdev and the IAF were already working closely together on Sri Lanka, the two knew each other well and the usual channels were bypassed.

Sahdev then spoke to Ronen Sen, who subsequently called him to a meeting in the army operations room at South Block later in the morning, where the prime minister, who was on his way back from Calcutta, would be present. So by the time Banerjee called Sahdev to inform him of the attempted coup, he found a battle-ready and prepared official who asked him to attend the prime minister's meeting.

The morning was taken up with preparations. At 8.30 a.m. Group Captain Ashok Goel, then joint director (operations, transport and helicopters), was summoned to the office of the Vice-Chief of the IAF, Air Marshal N.C. Suri, where he was asked about the availability of the transport fleet. 'I promptly replied that five IL-76s and sixteen AN-32s [Soviet-made Ilyushin-76 and Antonov-32 transport aircraft] were at Agra, and another fourteen AN-32s could be brought from Jorhat to Agra by 1 p.m. He directed me to alert the fleet and be ready to launch the operations to the Maldives,' Goel recalls. He too was asked to attend the meeting in the army operations room at South Block.

~

All participants have different versions of the meeting but most agree on a few things. Rajiv Gandhi walked in with Sen and Sahdev; others present included the service chiefs, officers from the military and air operations staff, the defence secretary and the chief of the Research and Analysis Wing (R&AW). The first few minutes of the meeting were chaotic and noisy. In Ronen Sen's words, 'No one had any clear ideas and people were passing around tourist picture postcards of the Maldives to make sense of the place.'

The deputy minister for home, P. Chidambaram, suggested flying the commandos of the then newly formed elite National Security Guard (NSG), which was under his charge, to the Maldives but that proposal was firmly shot down by the army. The intelligence available was sketchy and the R&AW, in particular, had scant information on what was happening in the Maldives. In fact, it was the last to know of the attempted coup and said that the international airport at Hulhule, a deserted island fifteen minutes from Malé by boat, had been taken over (this turned out be false) and that hundreds of rebels were spread across the island nation.

The R&AW chief was 'given a shut-up call' by Sen, who was best informed about the developing situation in Malé. This was thanks to what Sen calls 'the longest telephone call ever made between India and the Maldives'.

That call came from Zaki, the Maldivian foreign secretary, to 7 RCR and was taken by Sen before he proceeded for the meeting at South Block. From his house, Zaki could see the rebels who had captured the telephone exchange across the street. As he was explaining the situation, Sen told him not to hang up because that would cause the lights on the exchange switchboard to go off, alerting the rebels. They would then track Zaki down and India's connection to the Maldivian government would be lost.

The phone at Zaki's house in Malé and the one at 7 RCR – in the office of Rajiv Gandhi's private secretary, Vincent George – thus remained off the cradle till the military operation ended, eighteen hours later. It became the Indian government's sole reliable source of information, and the only way in which they managed a limited coordination with the Maldivian agencies.

As everyone settled into the meeting, Rajiv Gandhi summarized the crisis and referred to his visit to the Maldives in 1987. He noted that this was the first such request from a neighbour – an urgent SOS to save a regime from being overthrown by a coup. It was agreed that India must provide military help to the beleaguered government of the Maldives. India had never launched a military operation beyond Sri Lanka and its neighbours post-Independence. The Maldives campaign would thus be a first.

There was consensus that the army would have to take the lead in such a military operation – ground troops are the most effective way to seize military control in any battle. The air force would fly the army contingent in and keep its supply lines going. The navy was to remain on alert to respond to the evolving situation. The three services, Banerjee recalls, were confident about going into action. The armed forces were already in the midst of an active – and rather fierce – campaign in Sri Lanka and were in a state of preparedness to act promptly.

The discussion then came down to brass tacks – troop numbers, arms, aircraft, etc. There was no real information about the number of rebels, their weaponry or the backup available to them. Because shoulder-fired stinger missiles were being used by the mujahideen against the Soviet forces in Afghanistan to bring down helicopters and low-flying aircraft, there was a worry that these rebels too could possess them. It was also not clear whether the international airport at Hulhule was under the rebels or the government forces.

It was agreed that soldiers would be sent out from the Parachute Regiments – trained for landing in hostile terrain, being self-reliant and taking quick, effective action in tough conditions – for the operation. The 50 (Independent) Parachute Brigade, popularly called the Para Brigade, located at Agra is the only one of its kind in India. Because of its special training and unique role, this brigade is an army headquarters reserve, reporting to it directly.

The basic plan was simple. The soldiers, identifiable by their maroon berets and the parachute insignia on their uniforms, would be flown from Agra by the IAF within the next couple of hours and dropped by parachute at Malé to take out the rebels. But there was a hitch. The paratroopers needed a DZ – dropping zone – that was large enough to allow for the parachute drifting and still landing on firm ground.

But the Maldives is made up of islands with each island clustered into several islets. What the brigade needed was an island as large as a dozen football fields put together and Malé didn't qualify. Someone pointed out green patches at the periphery of the islands in the tourist maps as a possible DZ but these were coral reefs inside the sea, and not grassy fields.

There was no way the D5 parachute (the model used by the brigade) could be controlled while coming down from a height of 2500 feet in the air, with the drift provided by gentle sea winds. The chances of landing in the sea were high and the para battalions had never practised water-landing drills. On landing in water, a soldier would find it almost impossible to remove the harness and would most likely end up sinking like a stone.

Any landing in water – considering the dimensions of the island – would thus entail significant casualties. Rajiv Gandhi asked the army to quantify the possible casualties, and officers from the military operations directorate replied that this figure could be as high as 40 to 50 per cent. The plan was thus shelved – with the large number of body bags coming from Sri Lanka, it would have been a political, military and human disaster to have Indian soldiers die in the sea around the Maldives.

The plan then came around to landing the IL-76 aircraft at Hulhule airport. The Para Brigade would secure the airbase and use the commercial and private boats at the harbour to get to Malé. This took the discussion back to Hulhule airport. Ronen Sen's inputs, sourced from Zaki, suggested that the airport was still under the control of the government forces.

To add to the confusion, no one knew the size or had the plans of Hulhule airport even though it had been constructed by an Indian company. While efforts were being made to contact the company, Gandhi asked Sen to contact the Indian Airlines pilots who had been landing there regularly, as they would be best placed to provide the details.

Having been a commercial pilot himself, the prime minister was able to visualize the situation at the airport better than the others. He highlighted the various contingencies that could arise while landing at a place under rebel control. He suggested a tie-up with the Air Traffic Control (ATC) at Hulhule for a secret password or code word and for a quick signal, such as switching on the runway lights briefly as the first IL-76 approached the airport, to confirm that it was safe to land. Throughout the meeting, the prime minister remained remarkably calm and decisive.

With those details finalized, some decisions were made on how the mission was to be communicated. The United States was to be kept in the loop because its Diego Garcia base was only a few hundred flying miles from the southernmost atoll of the Maldives. There was to be no publicity till the Indian forces had landed in the Maldives, and the operation was to be projected as assistance to a friendly, democratic neighbour who had appealed to Delhi. The question of media coverage had not yet been broached but it took concrete shape later.

The urgency in the air heightened as the meeting concluded at 10.40 a.m. The political decision having been taken, it was now up to the forces to deliver. It was going to be a race against time if they were to save the Maldives and President Gayoom.

~

If the Maldivians had been caught with their pants down to their ankles on the night of 2–3 November, the Para Brigade's pants were at best at half-mast, wrote Brigadier Farooq 'Bull' Bulsara, the man who was then commanding the Para Brigade.

Bulsara is now no more but his principal staff officer, Major Vinod Bhatia, vividly remembers the scene at the headquarters in Agra on 3 November 1988. The brigade was busy preparing for its first administrative inspection, scheduled for the next day. The army had only recently decided to have an annual inspection for headquarters, a practice limited to battalions till then.

During an inspection, an independent team checks every document and office procedure to certify the unit. Most army officers liken this elaborate exercise, only half in jest, to their mother's visit home to inspect the wife.

Amid the flurry of preparations, Bulsara had gone to visit the Ordnance Park a few kilometres away. Bhatia remembers getting the first indication of an impending operation at around 10 a.m. when he got a call from Brigadier Malik at the military operations directorate telling him to ready one company group – around a hundred paratroopers with supporting elements like signals, engineers and medical teams – to move at six hours' notice and a battalion group – around 900 men – at twelve hours' notice.

The movement was to an island – no place was specified – and the soldiers had to be prepared for a beach assault. Bulsara was also ordered to reach Delhi by that evening for a meeting at the military operations directorate.

Assuming that this warning order must be for IPKF operations in Sri Lanka, Bhatia took out all the contingency plans, maps and aerial photographs of the strife-torn island. He also got Bulsara's vehicle ready to move to Delhi that evening. Malik's orders had come as a shock to Bhatia because the brigade's last major paradropping exercise, carried out a few weeks earlier, had been in very different terrain – the high-altitude environs of the Himalayas in the north-east, to send a signal to Chinese troops across the disputed border.

At 10.40 a.m., when the meeting chaired by Rajiv Gandhi at South Block had concluded, Bhatia got another call from Delhi, this time from the Vice-Chief of Army Staff, Lt Gen. S.F. Rodrigues. In the army, it is usually the staff officer who first comes on the line before transferring the call to the senior general. So Bhatia, who was expecting Rodrigues' staff officer to come on the line with the usual request for a paratrooper's jacket – an item of clothing popular with non-paratroopers – spoke rather curtly. To his surprise, it was Rodrigues himself. He said that one battalion group of paratroopers had to be ready to fly by twelve thirty that afternoon. The rest of the Para Brigade were to move later that night.

Rodrigues revealed that their destination was the Maldives, where an airborne assault had to be undertaken on an island beach. The enemy were identified as Sri Lankan Tamil militants who had automatic and anti-tank weapons, mortars and possibly some shoulder-fired surface-to-air missiles, or SAMs. Bhatia was told that the IAF had already allocated three IL-76 and ten AN-32 transport planes for the operation.

Bhatia tried to tell Rodrigues that none of the battalions of the brigade was in full strength at Agra and could not be mobilized in the next couple of hours. 7 Para had moved out on collective training to Band Baretha that morning at nine. Two of 6 Para's companies, out of a total of four, were on guard duty at the Agra Central Ordnance Depot after incidents of sabotage at some depots by Khalistan supporters. A company of 3 Para was out in Lucknow providing guards and security to the Command House and other establishments there. A tense, impatient Rodrigues cut Bhatia short, warning him that he would charge him with insubordination if he questioned his orders.

By this time Bulsara, alerted by Bhatia, had hurried

back to headquarters. His first reaction after his call with Rodrigues was, 'Now where in blazes is Maldives?'

Bulsara's intelligence officer brought out an atlas from the brigade library and indicated a cluster of islands, a few diminutive dots about 700 kilometres south-west of India's southernmost tip. He told Bulsara that those were the 1200 Maldivian islands, out of which about 200 were inhabited, fifty-odd as holiday resorts; that the country's political system was a single-party democracy; and that 98 per cent of the population was Muslim.

Meanwhile, Bhatia had sent a couple of officers to hotels and tourism bureaus in Agra to get whatever information they could on the Maldives. They returned with picture postcards and tourist brochures, and it was on the basis of these that the military operation was planned.

~

The IAF's main strategic transport base at Kheria in Agra, housing No. 44 Squadron with IL-76s, had been alerted by air headquarters at 7.15 a.m. to 'stand by for readiness 3 hours'. A conference was held in the squadron, with the flight commanders, their navigators, signals, engineers, gunner leaders and the squadron technical officer conducting their briefings. By 11 a.m., No. 44 Squadron under Wing Commander Anant Bewoor was ready and awaiting further instructions to fly the paratroopers to the Maldives. But the army felt that the IAF wasn't ready as the squadron was changing its plans by the minute and only three IL-76s were on the tarmac by then.

By noon, Bulsara had been briefed repeatedly over the telephone by Rodrigues, the director general of military operations and his deputy and had formed an initial plan. The battalion chosen to lead the operation was 6 Para, even though two of its companies were deployed to guard the Central Ordnance Depot. 3 Para, with the majority of its troops available in Agra, would have been the ideal choice, but the Commanding Officer (CO) of 3 Para, Col. K.L. Sharma, and Bulsara had a frosty equation. Sharma was a lifelong bachelor, a spiritual and rather ascetic man who spent his free time in meditation and prayer, while Bulsara was flamboyant, outgoing and gregarious. Bulsara got along better with Col. Subhash 'Joe' Joshi, the CO of 6 Para, and that is how Joshi's battalion was chosen to rescue the Maldivian President.

But there was a problem. The Central Ordnance Depot, under pressure to maintain its security, refused to release the two 6 Para companies guarding its premises. Soldiers from 10 Guards battalion at Babina, which was to take over the security duties at the Central Ordnance

Depot, would arrive at Agra only the following day. Bhatia recalls that the Central Ordnance Depot was told that withdrawal of the two companies of 6 Para was an operational requirement and 'these soldiers had orders to force the COD gate open, including by firing, if so required' to join the rest of their regiment. The threat worked. And 6 Para was soon on its way.

The initial plan, in Bulsara's words, was 'that a 6 Para company group would land at Hulhule, provided the airfield was still in loyal hands. In case an assault landing was not possible, the company would be paradropped to capture the Hulhule International Airport. Another company group, with my tactical headquarters, were kept ready as back-up.'

Because the plan was formed on the basis of rather sketchy inputs, Bulsara recounts, 'the decision to abort the mission, a rather ugly baby this, was left to me in case the rebels at Hulhule could not be tackled by this force. In that case we would have to launch a full-fledged airborne assault at first light the next day to capture the airfield.' This fresh assault was to take place from Trivandrum, the IAF base for the ongoing IPKF operations in Sri Lanka and the closest to the Maldives.

Just as the plans had begun to solidify, there was a fresh crisis. The IAF, which packs and holds the parachutes for the brigade, said that it had only sixty D5 packed parachutes. Although the IAF promised to make them available by next morning – Bulsara wondered 'how?'– it meant that a truncated company of 6 Para, instead of the full strength of 160 men, would have to be paradropped from an IL-76 on a beach south of Malé.

The aircraft take-off was scheduled for 2.30 p.m. but it didn't look like the brigade would make the deadline. Time was slowly ticking by. And with it the chances of success.

~

High Commissioner Banerjee in the meantime was racing to Agra along with senior army and air squadron officers to brief the IAF and Para Brigade with detailed orders, maps and the latest intelligence inputs. Banerjee recalls that when the prime minister's crisis meeting at South Block 'broke up around 11 a.m. I sought to make my way to the Ministry of External Affairs. General Raghavan [additional director general of military operations], out of the blue, came towards me and, putting his arm around me, wheeled me towards Foreign Secretary K.P.S. Menon and sought his permission to borrow me to brief the forces. Mr Menon did not think it was an unusual request and therefore agreed. I was then "handed over" to Brigadier V.P. Malik whose task it was to brief the Para Brigade in Agra.

'What happened next was simply extraordinary. Neither I nor, I am sure, the foreign secretary had any idea of what was to follow. Under the impression that the briefing would be in some other part of South Block, I followed the brigadier as he went quickly ahead. Soon we reached the Ministry of Defence gate on the southern side of South Block, which has the car park entrance. We were talking all the while, not really paying attention to much else. We got into a one-tonne military truck in which we were the only two passengers. Even at this stage I did not register the full implications of this journey. I thought we were headed towards Delhi Cantonment.'

And then reality hit. 'During the ride Brigadier Malik told me that we were going to Palam airport en route to Agra where the Para Brigade was stationed. All I could say to myself was, "Oh my gosh!"'

Banerjee still remembers every detail of that day. 'At the military apron in Palam airport we boarded an AN-12 which is basically a transport aircraft. Again, we were the only two occupants and we steadied ourselves by holding on to the hand grabs. It reminded me of my days as a student in Delhi University, journeying in DTC [Delhi Transport Corporation] buses; only, now there was no crowd and no jostling, but a lot of shaking and trembling as the aircraft took off and landed. At the Agra military airport we were taken by jeep to the Para Brigade headquarters to be greeted by a whole host of officers from both the army and the air force.'

By then it was already half past three in the afternoon. According to Bulsara, Banerjee 'had brought along a coffee-table travel book on the Maldives and a photo album with ten-odd photographs, which proved invaluable for us to plan the operation'. Malik had brought with him four photocopied tourist maps and sketches of Malé and Hulhule. Bhatia had been informed by the staff at the military operations directorate in Delhi that a wrong map had been sent by mistake, but no one was sure which one it was. At the joint briefing which was taking place at the 44 Squadron operations room at Kheria, the army and air force officers were briefed simultaneously. It was a clanging affair full of loud voices screaming over each other. Describing the scene, Bulsara wrote, 'The hideous cacophony of discordant voices there would have made a fish market appear serene.'

Among all the people present in that room, only Banerjee had been to the Maldives and knew the country first-hand. He was thus much in demand. 'After the army had their fill of me, it was the turn of the air force to check out a few things from the high commissioner. I was taken to another room where a large map was spread out on a table. 44 Squadron was seeking inputs for briefing their pilots. I couldn't stop looking at the map on the table in front of me. Somehow it didn't seem right.

'Then I realized what was wrong. Laid out on the table in front of me was not a map of Hulhule but of Gan, an airport 300 or so kilometres south of Malé. The near total lack of information for such a major international venture by India was woefully obvious.'

Banerjee still gets agitated thinking about that moment. Flinging the cap off his head, he says, 'I am not given to blowing my trumpet but I have often wondered what would have been the fate of this venture if I had not spotted the mistake. I almost shouted, more in relief than exasperation, that this was the wrong map. I explained that the Hulhule runway orientation was east–west while the map in front of me had a north–south orientation. The airport in Gan was a disused former RAF [Royal Air Force] base dating back to World War II. That our premier air force strategic airlift units flying the IL-76 were still dependent on these coordinates made me shiver. I confess my loud interjection had the desired impact and the Gan map was pushed aside while some officers rushed to bring the Hulhule map.'

Bulsara, meanwhile, had been updated on the little information Malik had brought: Malé was controlled by the mercenaries, numbering between 150 and 400; the Maldivian National Security Service comprising the land forces, the two-plane air force, coastguards and even customs were besieged in their headquarters and would not be able to hold out beyond evening; the President was hiding in a safe house, but nobody knew where; Hulhule international airport was functional and not in rebel hands.

Bulsara had also been told of the dropping zone that had been selected for his paratroopers, those with the sixty packed parachutes provided by the IAF. It was dangerously close to the sea, besides being far too small. Bulsara flatly rejected that option. Another dropping zone was suggested, a football field in the middle of Malé surrounded by high-rise buildings. It was nearly as bad.

Bulsara recounted it thus: 'The drop in this case, he said, would have to be in "sticks" of two from the front port exits only! I had had enough by then, so Vinod, Chuck [Colonel Chakraborty] and I started building on our original plan.'

～

As with any military operation, Bulsara's first step was to task his brigade. The task, according to him, was to rescue the President of the Maldives at the earliest. He decided to conduct the operation in four phases. In the first phase, 6 Para Battalion Group with its CO Joshi and a company – 160 men – of 3 Para would fly in an IL-76 to secure Hulhule airport. Two signals had been tied up with the ATC to indicate that the airport was still in the hands of loyal troops. On the first IL-76 establishing visual contact with the ATC, the runway lights would be switched on and then switched off immediately after a successful touchdown. The second signal was the password Hadiya, meaning 'guide to the righteous path', from the ATC to the IAF pilot to confirm that the airport was in safe hands.

In case of light opposition at Hulhule airport, sixty soldiers would be paradropped to capture the airfield and facilitate air landing operations. At this point, Bulsara said that he would be jumping with the soldiers and Bhatia insisted that he too be allowed to do so, to which Bulsara agreed. To have the brigade commander and his main staff officer jump with the first team is unheard of but that was what Bulsara was like – a daredevil who always led from the front.

In the second phase, a company of 6 Para would move by boat to secure a beachhead – a foothold on land – south-west on the Malé island and detach their high risk mission team to locate, rescue and secure President Gayoom. Another company of 6 Para would hold the airfield and push out a platoon to strengthen the company holding the Malé beachhead. A second 3 Para company of 160 men would hold the Hulhule jetty, round up all the country craft or dhonis and feign a head-on landing at the main jetty at Malé's Marine Drive to divert the mercenaries' attention from the beachhead.

In the third phase, the rest of the Para Brigade was to build up at Hulhule and 3 Para would reinforce 6 Para, if required. The last phase would involve getting President Gayoom to safety and mopping up the remaining mercenaries from the islands.

For all his flamboyance and cocksure attitude, Bulsara was gripped with self-doubt. 'All may seem neat and simple, but will we find an adequate number of country boats to ferry the troops across the 15-kilometre open stretch of sea to establish the beachhead; and if we did, would we be able to organize enough boat-men to navigate and man these boats? I'd be damned if anything would go wrong.'

He was equally worried about the fate of the sixty paratroopers if they had to use their parachutes to land at Hulhule airport. 'One look at an aerial photograph of the airfield in the Maldives tourist book was enough to rate the chances of survival of my 60 paratroopers at 70:30.

'Most paratroopers were bound to drift into the sea because there is precious little one can do to make a military parachute change its intended course of descent, and lesser still to carry out a water emergency drill or even get rid of the blooming thing, if one landed in the drink, fast enough before it became a rather outsized shroud and gave one a murderous dunking.'

Banerjee's impressions echo Bulsara's doubts. 'It soon became glaringly clear that our forces were at a tremendous disadvantage because of limited data. While our troops are trained to obey their superiors, and in moments of crisis never to withdraw, they at times take this to an extreme. It became all too evident in the discussions that took place with the brigade commander, Brigadier Bulsara, a tough, no-nonsense officer who asked searching questions. These related to when, where and how – the nitty-gritty of the ensuing operations. Ultimately the Paras were asked to improvise on the basis of the limited data, and the army headquarters expected them to do their best in the circumstances.'

Bulsara wanted Banerjee to fly with him to take advantage of the high commissioner's first-hand knowledge of the area. But Banerjee had different ideas. 'Late that afternoon, with the army and the air force finalizing their arrangements, I felt that I had fulfilled my purpose and I wanted to head home. But I was in Agra and there was no way I could get home until my hosts decreed that I could. Then came the biggest surprise of all – in a day full of surprises. Brigadier Malik asked if I would be interested in joining the operation.' Bulsara added his voice to the request.

'But I refused, stating that my role ended just where theirs was to begin. Brigadier Bulsara pointed out that this was a military-cum-political operation and had been so right from the first decision in Delhi. He added that by coming to Agra and by taking part in the joint briefing I had acknowledged that position. Appreciating his argument, I said that I would only get in the way since I was not a military professional. He scoffed at my words by saying that I thought like a military professional. We had a long discussion but I remained adamant. Finally, he said that we all had to serve the country in our own way. At this point I relented but gave two conditions before proceeding further.'

Banerjee's first condition was that the army headquarters had to secure official approval from the Ministry of External Affairs. His second condition was that he needed a razor as he always started his day with a shave and could not contemplate the next morning without one.

The first condition was easily fulfilled. For the second, Bulsara ordered his officers to have the army's canteen opened, and a suitable shaving kit including a toothbrush and towel was brought for his use.

'So when the troops of 50 Para Brigade started

boarding the two IL-76 aircraft complete with their assault rifles and other weapons, I boarded the lead aircraft complete with my shaving gear,' Banerjee recalls with a chuckle.

~

While the broad plan had been outlined by Bulsara, it was left to Bhatia to tie up the other details. Bhatia asked 6 Para to be ready by 3 p.m. inside the first IL-76 plane along with sixty D5 parachutes. Close on its heels would be the second IL-76 carrying one company of 3 Para, along with sappers, who were needed to operate the local country boats.

The IAF's original estimates were for a much bigger contingent and they had planned accordingly, but now seeing the reduced load, one aircraft was dropped from their plan of three IL-76s. While these decisions were being taken, the pilots passed the orders to uprate the fuel in all three aircraft which were to fly directly from Agra to Hulhule and remain on the ground at Hulhule with engines running for a short time before taking off for the return to Trivandrum. The take-off from Agra as scheduled for 4 p.m. but there was confusion till the last minute.

There was pressure from Delhi too, with the IAF Vice-Chief calling up Goel, who had been sent from Delhi along with the brigadier, every half-hour between 2 p.m. and 5 p.m., asking, 'What is the delay?' Goel says, 'The delay took place as 6 Para troops, the first load, arrived only at around 3.30 p.m. And the two IL-76 aircraft were readied only by 5 p.m.'

~

Group Captain A.K. Chordia was a parachute jump instructor (PJI) posted at Agra. On 3 November, he was supposed to lead a team to his alma mater, the National Defence Academy at Pune, for a skydiving demonstration. Their flight got delayed and was eventually cancelled and they were asked to await further orders. The new destination was unknown to them – all they were told was that it was an operational requirement.

Chordia thought that they must be going to Sri Lanka. Even when he boarded the aircraft, he thought they would be stopping over at either Trivandrum or Sulur, near Coimbatore, from where all the flights to Sri Lanka were launched. It is mandatory for thirteen PJIs to be on board an IL-76 during para-jumping operations. But this aircraft had only nine, among whom Chordia was the only officer.

Chordia recalled that 'the whole afternoon, there was an unusual bustle on the tarmac facing 44 Squadron.

Trucks and jeeps were surging past, carrying troops toting arms and equipment. PJIs could be heard shouting instructions. The ILs were guzzling fuel. The ground crew clinging to the various parts of the aircraft were busy carrying out their checks as the air crew moved to the two aircraft.'

Bewoor, CO of 44 Squadron, says, 'There had not been much time for detailed planning between 50 Para Brigade and 44 Squadron. Our charts were not current and the most reliable source of information was the tourist book on the Maldives given to us.'

The next hiccup to be encountered, with Goel and Bewoor as pilots and the planes ready to take off at around 4.45 p.m., is best described in Chordia's words: 'Settled in the cockpit, Goel and Bewoor started their pre-flight checks. In the other aircraft, the cacophony of the cargo compartment was interrupted by the crackling of the PA system. It also broke the chain of thought of Brigadier Bulsara. He was surprised that his aircraft would be the second one to take off. He sent me running to Goel in the other aircraft with a request to change the order, and put his aircraft in the lead. A negative response did not budge Brigadier Bulsara who emphasized the operational necessity of his aircraft reaching the objective first.'

Bulsara then sent Bhatia along with Chordia to convince Goel. 'I don't know what transpired between

Vinod Bhatia and the Air Force but the Air Force followed our plan,' Bulsara recalled. 'I am not very keen to find out how Vinod managed to convince the IAF, because he is always a company commander at heart and has never forgiven himself for being a ruddy staff officer when he ought to have been leading his company to rescue the President of Maldives, and is a less tolerant and a less patient man who tends to give expression to his emotions by swinging with his fists!'

Chordia recalls, however, that Bhatia used logic rather than his fists to persuade Goel: 'Bhatia told Goel that all the decision-makers were in the other aircraft and their whole plan depended on that aircraft landing first. A change in sequence would mean the plans going awry. Goel smartly manoeuvred past the imbroglio by interchanging the crew of the two aircraft. This is highly unusual and in fact unheard of.'

A few minutes before 5 p.m., as the sun set on the sleepy, smog-filled city of the Taj, Friendly One and Friendly Two rose above the horizon to fly over 2000 kilometres beyond the south-western coast of India towards the remote Indian Ocean archipelago. The paratroopers loudly hailed 'Chhatri Mata ki Jai' (Victory to the Goddess Parachute). Operation Cactus was on.

~

After the aircraft had climbed to their cruising altitudes and commenced level flight, activity among the soldiers reached a fever pitch in the cargo compartment of Friendly One. In the hour that the plane took to fly over Secunderabad, Bulsara had briefed the officers using the photographs in Banerjee's Maldives coffee-table book. Bhatia had hastily ordered transparency slides of the objectives of various companies, which were used to explain the tasks to the respective commanders. The glossy book on the Maldives was passed around. Photographs of President Gayoom were shown to the high risk mission team which was tasked to rescue him from the safe house.

After Bulsara's briefing, there was enough time left for the officers to brief their men in the cargo compartments. 'I was amazed to see travel magazines and tourist brochures on the Maldives instead of the familiar quarter-inch military maps in the hands of the man in fatigues while discussing the nitty-gritty of a military operation,' says Chordia. It was only once he was in the aircraft that he came to know that they were destined for the Maldives.

There was finally a lull in the feverish activity, and Banerjee was able to gather his thoughts more clearly. 'Once in the aircraft, I not only realized the enormity of the situation but also realized I was hungry. I had not eaten anything throughout the day.'

Meanwhile, Bulsara had eased himself into a

comfortable deckchair to catch up on some sleep, a lesson he had learnt well in his younger days as a para-commando. 'I believe that exhaustion usually results from failure to sleep when there is a chance. Combat effectiveness also is affected because of sleeplessness, a common phenomenon in the battlefield.'

The flight had been smooth so far. 'We were using civil air routes and were able to climb to 37,000 feet by the time we reported over Bangalore. In the Bangalore to Trivandrum sector, there were many thunderstorms below us. These troubled the escort Mirages and AN-32s on their way to Trivandrum,' Bewoor remembers.

Just out of Indian airspace, Bhatia says, there was an interception by a British Airways flight and the IAF plane had to reveal its destination. That is how the BBC was able to announce in its 7 p.m. bulletin that India was launching a military operation in the Maldives to save the president. Though many people speak of that BBC bulletin, tracing someone who had personally heard it proved impossible.

The families at Agra, meanwhile, were in the dark about the mission. Chordia had recently married and his wife believed that her husband was on his way to Pune. Bhatia's wife was used to her husband suddenly leaving for destinations unknown to her, and didn't bother to ask where and why. But she remembers something unusual happening that afternoon. It was the only time in Bhatia's service that his young son, who is now a paratrooper himself, stood in front of the jeep and asked his father not to go.

Mrs Bhatia became aware that something was afoot when their neighbour called them over to watch the Doordarshan news bulletin at 9 p.m., which announced that the Para Brigade was going to the Maldives. They were up all night counting the aircraft flying out from Agra. She says she counted around thirty-five of them fly over their quarters that night.

~

An hour short of Hulhule, Chordia saw a man in civvies sitting quietly at the rear of the cockpit. Curious, he approached him and discovered it was High Commissioner Banerjee. Chordia was keen to record memories of that eventful day. 'Even as the atmosphere became more and more tense as we approached the Maldives, I realized that it was a rare opportunity for me to be associated with an operation of that nature and magnitude. I flipped open my scribble pad and asked the high commissioner, "Sir, please pen down your thoughts for me." Mr Banerjee obliged with "I hope that everything goes off as planned."'

Banerjee says that except for the discussions with Bulsara and his officers, he was quiet and contemplative throughout the flight. 'Looking back, I don't recall any sense of fear on board the flight, even though we were on our way to offer aid and assistance through a military operation to a foreign country in an uncertain environment – and there were more uncertainties than certainties.'

Chordia then approached Bulsara, who was deep in thought, and asked him, 'Sir, what is uppermost in your mind?' and flashed his diary. Bulsara wrote, 'By 1000h tomorrow, we will secure the President and the airstrip.' Chordia could not muster the courage to go to the pilot, Group Captain Goel, with a similar request as he was flying the aircraft.

Before Chordia approached him, Bulsara had been woken up by Bhatia to take perhaps the most important operational decision of his life. Bhatia constantly revisits this moment – when Bulsara had to choose between paradropping sixty soldiers at the airfield or landing the aircraft – to highlight Bulsara's decision-making ability and why he is such an icon for him.

Bulsara too would write of it. 'Bhatia informed me that we would soon make visual contact with Hulhule and that Bewoor wanted my decision as to whether we "drop" Dhillon and his company first or attempt a landing.

53

Just then the code word "Hadiya" came over. In retrospect, I would say, any commander who has not faced his moment of truth has not really enjoyed that exhilaration which follows a decision rightly made. I faced mine at about 2125 hours over the Indian Ocean and now I can justifiably say that I took the right decision.'

There were a few things going through Bulsara's mind. 'Even then one was not certain whether or not a rebel was holding a pistol to the ATC man's head. All it would take for an operation to end up in a terrible mess was to lure us in for a landing and roll a bowser across the runway just after we touched down. That would be the end of the show.'

Bhatia remembers Bulsara closing his eyes for a minute, thinking about it, and then boldly giving his reply. But that is not how Bulsara saw it later. 'I don't recollect weighing any pros and cons, but just telling Anant Bewoor to go in and land.'

It was all now in the hands of the two pilots, Goel and Bewoor. Bewoor recounts, 'We were about 25 kilometres from touchdown when we asked for runway lights; they came on for about ten seconds and were switched off, but we had quickly aligned with the runway. The IL-76's navigation computer, Kupol, guided us and we continued our descent towards a dark, unlit runway, smack in the middle of the dark ocean.'

Complicating matters further was the coral sea surrounding Hulhule. 'No further radio telephony transmissions were made after the initial identifications were established. Our mapping radar KP-3 was now picking up an enormous echo because the coral sea was so shallow that it painted on the radar screen. The exact position of the runway could not be ascertained. Nor did we have any kind of perspective to adjust our descent and approach path,' Bewoor explains.

'At about 200 metres above sea level, indicated on the radio altimeter, I transmitted "Lights". They came on, we flared out, chopped power and as the tyres touched the concrete, runway lights were switched off.' Bewoor remembers the touchdown vividly.

It was pitch-dark and, after a short run, the IL came to a standstill, the aft-end ramp was lowered and in no time the 150 men and two jeeps were out. It was 9.48 p.m.

'So far so good,' Bulsara thought.

Bhatia believes that this was the most critical part of the operation. He and his boss, Bulsara, could never be sure that the person at the Hulhule ATC had not been compromised or coerced by the rebels or that they were not walking into a trap laid by the Tamil mercenaries. The army was at that time beset with stories of the Tamil Tigers cunningly leading soldiers into a trap, often resulting in heavy casualties. That context shaped their fears, even as Bulsara boldly chose to come in the first aircraft and then to land at Hulhule airport.

As the aircraft was being emptied quickly to allow the second aircraft to land, Malik asked Banerjee whether he would like to return with him on the plane to Bangalore or remain in the Maldives.

'I didn't hesitate. I said that he could go back but I was going to stay,' Banerjee recalls. 'In my mind, I was clear; I had returned to my charge where in my absence there had been an attempted coup, and the matter still needed attention and I was going to be part of this action.'

The eagle had landed. A flight of four hours and forty-four minutes from wheels up at Agra to the runway at Hulhule had safely touched down, within just sixteen hours of the first phone call being received in Delhi from the Maldives. It was time for some live action.

~

The Indian high commissioner by his side, Bulsara was now in the thick of the action. There were sounds of sporadic gunfire and the occasional thud of high explosives coming from a distance. In the melee of soldiers rushing out, he had been separated from Bhatia. The other officers, thoroughly briefed, were all on their way to their assigned tasks. The initial parties fanned out to secure the airport and the terminal. As the first aircraft turned around and took off, the second IL-76 landed, and took off less than five minutes later. The troops from the second plane secured the ATC, jetty, fuel jetty and the northern and southern ends of the airfield.

Through some tall grass and broken ground, Bulsara headed for the terminal building along with his batman and the radio operator. He found Bhatia there, along with the officers who had landed in the second aircraft. Bhatia informed Bulsara that one of their teams had just beaten a group of mercenaries to the jetty, who were even then attempting to land there and take control of the boats.

This was one of the what-ifs that had worried Bulsara and his team – the journey to Malé. What if there were no dhonis at Hulhule, or what if there were no boatmen? They would then have had to wait for the army boats to fetch up in one of the later flights. That would have delayed the operation and handed over the advantage to the mercenaries.

Chordia, who had got down along with another colleague to guide a paradrop over a dropping zone if required later, moved to the ATC. As soon as the troops had control of the ATC, they tried to establish radio contact with the president at his secret location in Malé. This was done through a loyal Maldivian official at the

ATC who had transmitted the password to the IL-76 and switched on the runway lights for landing.

Banerjee was the first to speak to the president. 'I greeted the president briefly, and informed him that India had taken immediate steps to come forward to help him in response to his urgent appeal. I then handed the mike to Brigadier Bulsara.'

The president implored Bulsara to hurry up, as the rebels had surrounded his safe house and he could hear firing close by. Bulsara told the president, 'Mr President, the Indian army has arrived and will do its best.'

In that short conversation, Bulsara had actually underplayed his determination to save the president. 'I was not about to go through what I had these past ten hours, fly 3000 kilometres, and then lose him to a bunch of ragtag mercenaries.'

He was determined to have the troops move quickly to Malé and Banerjee's presence turned out to be of great help there. Some Maldivian National Security Service officials who had secured the airport during the day but had discarded their uniforms to merge with the crowd now emerged from the darkness. Banerjee recognized a couple of them who were normally deployed at the president's office and the ministry of foreign affairs. More important, several of them recognized Banerjee and that made the paratroopers' task easier, as they arranged dhonis from the jetty and also acted as guides and boatmen for the route to Malé.

Every successful military operation requires more than a dose of luck, and the Para Brigade had been lucky with a couple of things so far. The rebels had not thought of capturing Hulhule airport, and dhonis were available at Hulhule to take the soldiers to Malé. In addition, Banerjee's presence had helped them find guides and boatmen.

~

The plan for the beach assault at Malé had also been firmed up. Having encountered little rebel presence at Hulhule, Bulsara decided to dispatch from the airport one company of 6 Para under Major R.J.S. Dhillon, to secure a beachhead south-west of Malé. Joshi, CO of 6 Para, was to follow Dhillon and take control of the operations at Malé, while Bulsara remained at Hulhule. Simultaneously, a platoon of 3 Para under Captain R.D. Poonakar was to launch a diversionary attack towards the main jetty at Malé at Marine Drive where firefights were taking place.

This was to draw the rebels towards Poonakar while Dhillon's company established a beachhead and rescued the president. Dhillon was then tasked, along with two high risk mission teams, to accompany the president to a safe area at Hulhule airfield while the rest of the forces tackled the rebels at Malé.

Using an assortment of boats, the beachhead assault was set in motion. Dhillon's men had boarded four launches and set course over the open sea, with Dhillon at the head in the first launch. Poonakar's men made for the Marine Drive jetty in two boats. As they sailed two kilometres across the open sea, they reamined faintly visible to the naked eye from Hulhule.

Poonakar was not supposed to land at the jetty. It was a diversionary tactic. But watching them edge too close to the jetty, Bulsara 'had a nasty feeling that he had got my orders wrong and was attempting a landing to capture it!' And then he heard the gunshots. The mercenaries at the jetty were shooting. Poonakar's men needed no second invite – they had been waiting for this moment for ten hours.

It was all guns blazing from the two launches. From the machine-gunners to the riflemen, everyone kept their fingers on the trigger – contrary to all their training – and the two boats pumped bullets at the jetty. The shock of the lead unloaded on the jetty was far too much for the mercenaries. About 50 metres short of the jetty, Poonakar's launches swung outwards and turned back towards Hulhule for a second run-in.

Bulsara had asked President Gayoom to position guides where the rescue teams led by Dhillon could be directed once the beachhead was established. Dhillon's team at first lost their bearings but eventually managed to land without opposition and establish a beachhead. Their boats returned to Hulhule to bring Joshi and another company to build up on the beachhead.

Meanwhile, President Gayoom had called Bulsara and asked him to hurry up. His position was becoming untenable and he could not remain in the safe house much longer without being discovered. Bulsara assured him that his men were already in Malé, and they would get him to safety in no time.

Wary of the radio communication being intercepted by the rebels, Bulsara was not keen to pass on the location of the guides to Dhillon over radio. The Maldivian National Security Service lieutenant who had recognized Banerjee and had accompanied Dhillon on the boat guided him to the house of the Maldivian deputy defence minister, who had been injured in the day's fighting earlier. The deputy defence minister provided Dhillon a guide to the president's safe house. But when Dhillon and his men reached there, the president's security guards were extremely jittery and refused to give Dhillon's party access.

Bulsara's patience was being tested by the second by

these reports. 'It took about half an hour to convince the NSS men about our intentions and, now almost at the end of my tether, I was about to order Dhillon to shoot his way in and secure the president, when better-sense prevailed upon the guards and they let our men go through.'

At 2.10 a.m. on 4 November, the Maldivian President was finally secured by the paratroopers of the Indian army. Dhillon and Joshi tried to persuade President Gayoom to move to Hulhule. The president flatly refused. He instead wanted to be taken to the National Security Service headquarters.

'I was the most lonely and worried man till I received news of President Gayoom being rescued; because once he has committed his troops, a commander is, of necessity, a solitary man with virtually nothing to do. He carries an enormous burden of responsibility and he carries it alone,' wrote Bulsara later of this moment.

Unlike in any other military operation, where a commander reports to a superior commander, Bulsara was totally on his own, thousands of miles away from any of his senior officers. The buck stopped with him. Even though he may not have realized it then, India's reputation as a regional power rested on his broad shoulders.

~

Bulsara's primary task of securing the president had been completed seven and a half hours ahead of his own target, but the situation in Malé was still not under control. He decided to push the rest of the 6 Para battalion to Malé, while Hulhule was given to 3 Para which had fetched up in one of the sixty sorties flown by the IAF that night. These IL-76s, AN-32s and AN-12s had brought in the rest of the Para Brigade and an army field hospital to the Maldives.

By dawn, the IAF had positioned a flight of Mi-8 helicopters to allow the quick ferrying of troops to chase the fleeing mercenaries across the islands. Mirage 2000 fighter aircraft, operating from Trivandrum, made low-level passes over a number of Maldivian islands in a show of force.

Taken aback by the show of force and the amount of lead unleashed on them by the paratroopers, many mercenaries surrendered. But some, including their leader Luthufi, took control of a ship, *MV Progress Light*, anchored at Malé harbour, along with a score of hostages, including a Maldivian minister. Luthufi forced the ship to set sail around the time Dhillon entered the National Security Service headquarters.

Banerjee claims to have detected the moving ship first. 'I spotted a whole set of lights gently, ever so slowly, moving to our left. It suddenly occurred to me that this was a ship moving out of the harbour. Brigadier Bulsara and I had got separated in the meantime and so I shouted out to him that a ship was moving out of the harbour. It was past midnight, and it aroused my suspicions immediately. Brigadier Bulsara agreed that it was indeed a ship, probably the one that had ferried the mercenaries from Sri Lanka, and that it was now trying to get away.'

Bulsara watched the ship sailing head-on towards Hulhule from the Malé harbour about four kilometres to the east of the island. It was lit up too brightly, and as it sailed in parallel to Hulhule, the ship presented Bulsara's men a tempting target. He ordered the troops on the perimeter facing the sea channel to open fire. The medium machine guns opened up, as did the Carl Gustav rocket launcher teams, which fired four rounds. By then the ship had picked up speed and sailed out of range.

A dismayed Bulsara swore loudly at his men for missing. But all was not lost. Captain N.S. Ghei, stationed on the southern side of the island, had seen the black silhouette of the ship – which had by now switched off all its lights – moving from left to right, and radioed Bhatia. Bhatia asked him for the ship's distance from his position. Ghei replied that he could not estimate this because of the darkness and the sea. Bhatia asked

Ghei to wait as he thought things out. Then he ordered: 'Fire, and fire.'

Ghei initially opened fire with his carbine Sten gun, which has a range of barely 50 yards, and then with the light machine gun which has a range up to 400 metres. Meanwhile, his intelligence JCO came with a shoulder-fired Carl Gustav 84mm rocket launcher used to shoot at tanks. Ghei and the JCO ran along the beach and were able to fire three high-explosive rounds. One of them ricocheted off the water and hit the ship's steering mechanism, locking the steering wheel.

This forced *MV Progress Light* to travel only in a straight line, and prevented it from getting into any commercial shipping lane. Once inside a shipping lane, it could easily merge with hundreds of other commercial ships, making it impossible to identify from the air. By then, Bulsara had ordered that the ship's coordinates be sent out by wireless to the naval base in Goa so that they could take further follow-up action. The ship moved in a south-south-westerly direction, heading towards the Straits of Malacca passage.

~

Meanwhile, at Malé, Captain M.K. Singh of 6 Para was given the responsibility of securing the president and his family at the safe house while Dhillon moved with additional forces to the National Security Service headquarters. It was still surrounded by mercenaries though their leaders had fled. In the firefight that ensued, the siege of the NSS headquarters was lifted. Simultaneously, the Marine Drive jetty was secured at Malé after an exchange of fire with the rebels.

The NSS had sent a speedboat to fetch Bulsara from Hulhule. He put on his helmet and Banerjee too joined him in wearing one. Bulsara sought to dissuade Banerjee from going with him, but the high commissioner insisted. They landed at the Malé beachfront at 3 a.m., after what he described as 'a rather harrowing 15-kilometre boat ride during which the Maldivian Coast Guard at the helm was hell-bent on breaking all water speed records, with the prow constantly slapping down hard as we crested wave after wave'.

At about 3.15 a.m., Bulsara and Banerjee entered the NSS headquarters, where M.K. Singh had just escorted the President. A score of dead bodies, mostly of the rebels and mercenaries, lay around the building. The pockmarked walls bore ample proof of the mercenaries' dogged attempts to break in and of the NSS men's equally determined efforts not to let them in.

Banerjee remembers that the president 'looked shaken but was in full command, and was happy to receive us. He had with him his foreign minister and one or two others. He thanked us for the timely help and said he wanted to speak to the PM, Rajiv Gandhi.'

The satellite telephone link between Delhi and Malé was still functional and at 4 a.m. President Gayoom spoke to Rajiv Gandhi from the NSS headquarters. He thanked him for the timely assistance, telling him that the Indian soldiers were in full control of Malé. Ronen Sen recalls that Gandhi was at that time working on his desktop computer – 'typing with one finger as he always did' – and it was only after this call with President Gayoom that he went to sleep.

As a concession to Sen's long day, the prime minister told him he could come late to office. But Sen's relief was short-lived. "'Come by 9.30 or so," Rajiv said, and added, "and do get the draft of the document I had asked you to prepare,"' Sen recalls wryly. As Sen left Rajiv's study, his last instruction was, 'Do congratulate the defence minister [K.C. Pant] on my behalf for a successful operation.' But he added with a smile, 'Leave it; he might be asleep.'

~

While the prime minister and his team in Delhi had finally called it a day, the mopping-up operations continued at Malé. Bulsara moved 3 Para to Malé, and at 5 a.m. he asked the president to order all the National Security Service personnel to get into their uniforms. Having earlier discarded their uniforms, when the rebels seemed to have the upper hand, these men were now roaming around with weapons, causing much confusion among the paratroopers. So Bulsara froze the operations till 7 a.m. to allow all the NSS men to put on their uniforms.

Meanwhile, after meeting the president, Banerjee took leave of Bulsara and went for a walk around Malé. He saw evidence of the night's battle everywhere: some dead bodies, empty bullet casings and garbage strewn all over the streets. As news of the Indian forces' arrival spread and the Maldivians learned that their president was safe, Banerjee saw people come out of their homes and line the streets, expressing their gratitude, waving and clapping. He headed for the high commission, took over his duties and phoned his wife in Delhi to tell her what had happened over the past sixteen hours. That was the first time he had spoken to her since the previous morning. His staff and secretary were happy to have their boss back in the saddle.

With the mopping-up operations frozen by Bulsara between 5 a.m. and 7 a.m., it became evident that there was a mini crisis for breakfast – there had been no time in the night to set up kitchens for the troops and food rations and kitchen equipment were still being flown out from India. By now there were 1600 Indian troops in the Maldives, as well as a large party of journalists and cameramen who had landed at 3 a.m. The journalists, accompanied by Partha, stayed in the Maldives for a couple of hours and then flew back to Delhi.

President Gayoom ordered whatever was available at Hulhule airport to be provisioned for the Indian soldiers. The water desalination plant at Malé was not functioning, so now, instead of ammunition and weapons, the administrative party of the Para Brigade focused on sending water through various IAF aircraft flying to Malé.

The operations were to recommence at 7 a.m. but 4 November was a Friday and, as the Maldives is an Islamic republic, the president requested that they be called off for that day. Bulsara was reluctant, as this would give the mercenaries the opportunity to escape, but had to agree. The paratroopers had by then accounted for some thirty-odd mercenaries and captured a large quantity of arms and ammunition. To prevent any rebels from escaping while the operations were suspended, they established a cordon at sea around Malé, using an assortment of country boats and launches.

The first rebel boat to be apprehended was when a team of 6 Para, moving from Hulhule to Malé, spotted a suspicious-looking boat heading for Dhunidoo Island. Subedar Pritam Singh, leader of the team, chased the boat as it started speeding towards the high seas. There was a brief firefight before the paratroopers boarded the boat. Four well-armed mercenaries, all Sri Lankan Tamils, were apprehended and brought to Malé for interrogation.

By then, the VIP military visits from India had started. Every senior military official from Southern Command and from Delhi wanted to be part of the successful operation and this put some strain on Bulsara, who wasn't exactly known for being tactful and polite at the best of times. He was criticized for taking the call to land, putting everyone's life at risk. Later on a senior army official wrote to him, cautioning him about his rude behaviour.

At 8 a.m. on 5 November, Bhatia informed Bulsara that a US task force from its base in Diego Garcia – comprising three cruisers, one landing platform helicopter and one British destroyer – was about four hours away and wanted permission to harbour at Malé. This flotilla had set sail in response to the Maldivian President's request for help but was approaching when the Indians had already finished the operation. The American task force was denied permission to harbour at Maldives and returned to Diego Garcia.

~

MV Progress Light, with top mercenary leaders and seven hostages including the Maldivian minister and his Swiss mother-in-law, was still at sea. On the evening of 5 November, an IL-38 of the Indian Navy landed at Malé. On board was Commander Naik, who was the navy's chief liaison officer to Bulsara. Naik was informed about the ship that had sailed away after being fired at.

Armed with a rough sketch of the ship and the general direction of its movement, the IL-38 spotted it about 60 kilometres off Malé, listing heavily to the starboard side. When the pilot made a low pass, the ship changed course abruptly, confirming Naik's suspicions.

The navy directed *INS Godavari*, which was returning from a goodwill visit to Australia and New Zealand, to intercept *MV Progress Light*. The ship was commanded by Captain S.V. Gopalachari, who was in a hurry to get back home after eighty-two days at sea for his wife's birthday on 8 November. But the message from headquarters changed his plans abruptly. The training frigate *INS Betwa* was also directed to assist *INS Godavari* in the operation.

Sushil Kumar, then director of naval operations and later Navy Chief Admiral, recounts, 'As the drama unfolded at sea, the Indian Navy operations room in Delhi was palpably tense yet privileged by the presence of Prime

Minister Rajiv Gandhi, who was keenly following the action. The Maldivian President had personally requested that the rebels be captured and brought back to Malé to face trial, so ensuring the safety of the hostages and also rounding up the rebels was certainly going to be a daunting task.'

The November 1988 issue of *India Today* magazine quotes Gopalachari as saying, 'The first radio contact was made on the shippers' Channel 16 when we were still several miles away.' The mercenaries warned him to stay at least six miles away and threatened to kill the hostages if he came any closer. Since *MV Progress Light* only moved at six knots, the naval ships had no real problem keeping it tightly hemmed in even at a distance of two to three miles. Their main worry was that the mercenaries would get away on a faster speedboat which, at that range, could easily come in from the Sri Lankan shore.

After hours of inaction at sea, Sushil Kumar says, a terse message from the Sri Lankan Navy came like a bombshell to the Indian Navy operations room. 'The Sri Lankan Navy had been directed by its government to destroy the rebel ship, if it approached within 100 miles of the Sri Lankan coast. Our sources also confirmed that Sri Lankan Navy gunboats were manoeuvring out of the Colombo harbour.'

The Sri Lankan ultimatum posed an operational dilemma for the Indian Navy, since the rebels were hell-bent on taking the ship to Sri Lanka. The mandate given to the Sri Lankan Navy could have led to a naval confrontation resulting in the hostages being killed. Fortunately, a working relationship between the two navies formed due to IPKF operations in Sri Lanka helped defuse the situation.

But time was running out. Gopalachari was given a simple command: 'Stop *Progress Light*.' *INS Godavari* closed in to a distance of a little over a mile; the mercenaries aboard *MV Progress Light* retaliated by dragging two hostages to the bridge and blowing their heads away. Their bodies were strapped to lifebuoys and thrown into the sea in the hope that the gruesome sight would deter their pursuers.

Gopalachari told *MV Progress Light* that unless it surrendered, firing would begin. But the mercenaries pressed on, and *INS Godavari* opened up in right earnest. One of the first shells from the 30mm anti-aircraft cannons broke the foremast on *MV Progress Light*, prising away the ship's speedboat and, with it, the rebels' only hope of escape. A massive undersea explosion from a helicopter-dropped depth charge sent a spine-chilling shudder through the rebel ship.

'Shrapnel flew all over and at this point the mercenaries had begun to panic,' V.A. Vincent, the second officer of *MV Progress Light*, later told *India Today*. At least three mercenaries jumped into the water in panic. Unfortunately, four hostages were killed in the bargain.

Meanwhile, Gopalachari began to negotiate with the rebel leader Luthufi in Tamil, trying to persuade him to surrender while the task force of *Godavari* and *Betwa* fired on. Luthufi eventually gave in. Navy commandos stormed on board. Boats were lowered by the navy and the fit hostages were asked to jump in. The others were picked up later, along with the mercenaries.

'Hostages rescued safely and rebels captured' was the final message from *INS Godavari*. On 8 November, *INS Godavari* sailed into Malé with the rescued hostages, including the minister, the mercenaries and the rebels. President Gayoom received the hostages at Malé. Other wounded hostages, including the Swiss mother-in-law of the Maldivian minister, were flown to Trivandrum, and then to Pune for treatment.

As the operation ended and a smiling Rajiv Gandhi walked out of the operations room, he couldn't resist a wisecrack. 'Why did you have to save the mother-in-law? You could have done the minister at least that favour!'

~

The Para Brigade started withdrawing from the Maldives on 6 November and by 13 November all except 300 men from 6 Para and a platoon of sappers had flown back to Agra. These men stayed on for a year before returning to India. India engaged more actively with President Gayoom during this period, and Kuldip Sahdev, joint secretary (BSM), made several visits to the island country. Many development schemes were started in the Maldives, and among them, as Ronen Sen recounts, was the establishment of at least one more secure communication link between the two capitals.

Operation Cactus, as it was officially christened, was hailed internationally. British Prime Minister Margaret Thatcher commented, 'Thank God for India. President Gayoom's government has been saved. We could not have dispatched a force from here in good time to help him.' Congratulating India for thwarting the attempted coup in the Maldives, US President Ronald Reagan said this action 'will be remembered as a valuable contribution to regional stability'. *Time* did a cover story – thanks to Rajiv Gandhi's tip-off to Ross Amroe – 'Super Power Rising'. Even top military officials in Pakistan expressed their surprise and awe at the swiftness of India's response.

But the men who participated in the operation did not get any medal for it, as they usually do for all military operations, be it Kargil or Siachen or Sri Lanka. As the

Indian army was suffering heavy casualties in Sri Lanka at the same time, there would be hardly any gallantry awards for a flawless operation in the Maldives where Indian armed forces did not lose a single man. The defence ministry has still not brought out its official history of the operation, which was so well executed and lauded globally.

Looking back, the officials who played such an extraordinary role in the affair wonder why twenty-eight years later a more powerful and stronger India wouldn't even dream of embarking on such a courageous adventure any more, why the kind of swift and perfect coordination between all arms of the government that took place on that day no longer seems possible now.

The final accolade for Operation Cactus came from the mercenary leader Luthufi. After surrendering to the navy commandos, Luthufi told *India Today* aboard *INS Godavari*, 'Uma Maheswaran [head of PLOTE] approached me in my poultry farm near Colombo and asked me to take over the country.'

But did he really expect such a crazy, reckless venture to succeed, he was asked. 'Why not?' he shot back with chutzpah. 'Anyone can be the president of such a country. If only luck had been with us. If only the Indian troops had not come for a few more hours . . .'

Operation Pawan:
Massacre at Jaffna

When top LTTE commanders swallowed cyanide pills and killed themselves to avoid being handed over by the IPKF to the Sri Lankan government, the cordial relationship between the Indians and the LTTE turned frosty overnight. The IPKF was thrown head first into a vicious conflict with the rebels for which it was materially unprepared, without maps or artillery, and took casually at first. In a tragic miscalculation, Indian soldiers were heli-dropped into the LTTE's lair at Jaffna, where they suffered heavy casualties and, against all odds, fought their way out. The operation marked the start of a bloody conflict which, over the next thirty months, saw nearly 1200 Indian soldiers lose their lives.

It was 5 October 1987. The Palali military base, in northern Sri Lanka, was bustling with activity that afternoon. Indian soldiers, their weapons at the ready, milled around a single-storey building. Medium machine guns (MMGs) primed with hundreds of 7.62mm bullets had been positioned in the vicinity and a chain of grenades encircled the building: removing one pin off a grenade would start a series of blasts, unleashing a tornado of sound and destructive fury. The big guns of the armoured protective carriers of the IPKF were menacingly pointing towards the building, which housed seventeen LTTE prisoners.

These were no ordinary prisoners. They included two of the LTTE's top leaders: its Batticaloa commander, Pulendran, and its Trincomalee commander, Kumarappa. Pulendran was leader of the LTTE squad that had shot dead 126 Sinhalese bus passengers, including many children, at Habarana and Kithulotowa in April 1987, in one of the deadliest terror attacks in Sri Lanka. Kumarappa was the brother-in-law of the LTTE supremo Velupillai Prabhakaran. The men had been smuggling arms in their boat when they were arrested from Point Pedro in the Palk Straits by the Sri Lankan navy on 2 October and brought to Palali, where they were under IPKF custody, as the Indians, the neutral party, were umpiring between the LTTE and the Sri Lankan government.

At Palali the Indian army's 54 Artillery Brigade was administratively in charge of the prisoners. Commanded by Major General Harkirat Singh, 54 Airborne Division was then the de facto IPKF headquarters in Sri Lanka. Also present at the base were Sri Lankan soldiers and the 10 Para Commando battalion of the Indian army.

On 5 October the prisoners asked for some stationery, which was duly supplied by the soldiers of the 54 Artillery Brigade. Around noon came tiffin carriers with lunch for the prisoners. The Indian soldiers allowed in the food after cursory checks, as they had been doing the past three days. But that day they missed a crucial element in the lunch boxes. Buried in the food was something more potent than a Tamil curry: cyanide capsules.

At ten that morning, Major Sheonan Singh, leader of the para commandos team, had received orders from 54 Division to hand over the prisoners to the Sri Lankan army at 4 p.m. Sheonan's men had laid the MMGs and the grenades as a protective measure, to allow the Indian soldiers to safely leave the building after the handover.

The handing over of the LTTE prisoners to the Sri Lankans had been a contentious issue. The anti-India faction of the Sri Lankan government had demanded that the LTTE men be brought to Colombo for trial. The LTTE said that their men had been granted amnesty and would be tortured if taken to Colombo. The LTTE was hoping that the IPKF would not bow down to Sri Lankan pressure. After all, the Tamil cause in Sri Lanka – for which the LTTE had taken up arms – had been supported by India.

Sheonan understood the political consequences of the orders he had received. He pleaded with the military operations directorate at Delhi not to hand over the LTTE prisoners to the Sri Lankan army – it would lead to a dangerous rupture between the LTTE and the IPKF, and alienate Tamils, both in Sri Lanka and in India – but to no avail. Kumarappa, who overheard his conversation, asked Sheonan, 'Why are you doing this? Our leaders have told us that if we are handed over to the Sri Lankan army we will have our last meal and write our last letter.'

At the time, Sheonan didn't grasp the import of what Kumarappa had said; his words would come back to haunt him later.

He looked at his watch. It was 4 p.m. He walked up to the Sri Lankan colonel and, as he handed over charge of the LTTE prisoners to him, said, 'All yours and I wish you the best.' Sheonan then informed the Colonel GS – the principal staff officer to General Harkirat – over the wireless radio that the LTTE prisoners were now in the custody of the Sri Lankan army.

Sheonan and his men drove back to their base 500 metres away. Within a few minutes, a staff officer from Division HQ, which was within walking distance, came running. He told Sheonan to return to the building and take back custody of the prisoners from the Sri Lankans. An angry Sheonan retorted that he needed specific orders to do so. Minutes later the Colonel GS, who had taught Sheonan at Staff College in Wellington a couple of years earlier, came personally to ask him to take the prisoners back from the Sri Lankans.

Sheonan's response was: 'Am I to open fire if Sri Lankans don't hand the prisoners back? What am I to do if Sri Lankans open fire on the LTTE prisoners? What if both sides fire on each other?' He wanted explicit orders to cover all these contingencies. The Colonel GS tried to get through to the military operations directorate at Delhi for answers, but it was already too late. While he was on the phone, Sheonan got a wireless message from the Sri Lankans: Pulendran, Kumarappa and the other prisoners had swallowed cyanide pills. And thirteen of them were dead.

The suicide of the prisoners turned the LTTE bitterly and violently against India and the IPKF. The vacillation by New Delhi on 5 October 1987 was to cast a long, dark and bloody shadow, leading to the assassination of Rajiv Gandhi by the LTTE in May 1991. But the immediate consequence was a military debacle.

~

The LTTE were especially stung by what they saw as India's betrayal, because, for years, the Indian government had supported the Tamil demand for equal political rights in Sri Lanka. The LTTE itself had been bestowed with considerable largesse by New Delhi, which saw Prabhakaran and his band – funded, trained, supplied and guided by Indian intelligence agencies – as 'our boys'. The LTTE's record of murder and mayhem was no doubt chilling, but the organization, and the cause it represented, had substantial popular support in Tamil Nadu.

As recently as June 1987, the travails of Sri Lankan Tamils had weighed heavily on India's Sri Lanka policy. That month, Delhi announced it was sending a convoy of unarmed ships to northern Sri Lanka to provide humanitarian assistance to Tamils trapped in Jaffna, under siege by the Sri Lankan army. These ships were intercepted by the Sri Lankan navy and forced to return to India. Following the failure of the naval mission, Rajiv Gandhi decided to airdrop relief supplies for Tamils in Jaffna. This demonstrated India's concern for the civilian Tamil population and signalled to the Sri Lankan government that India could, if necessary, exercise the option of active Indian military intervention in support of Sri Lankan Tamils.

Having demonstrated his political will, Rajiv Gandhi signed the India–Sri Lanka accord with the Sri Lankan President, J. Jayewardene, on 29 July 1987, aimed at bringing peace to the island nation while ensuring Tamil rights. Under the terms of the agreement, Colombo agreed to a devolution of power to the provinces, the Sri Lankan troops were to be withdrawn to their barracks in the north and the Tamil rebels were to disarm. The LTTE was not a signatory to the accord and played a delicate balancing game for the first couple of months. It claimed to support the accord – it performed a symbolic surrender ceremony with some old weapons in early August – but insisted that the Sri Lankan government had not kept its part of the deal.

Under the mandate of the accord, an Indian military contingent called the Indian Peace Keeping Force was sent to Sri Lanka, primarily for policing duties. Major

General Harkirat Singh, who was commanding the Secunderabad-based 54 Airborne Division – which consisted of around 10,000 men – became the first commander of the IPKF, based at Palali. His troops left Secunderabad for Sri Lanka within six hours of the signing of the accord.

No detailed military planning was done while dispatching the troops from Secunderabad, as no one imagined that Indian soldiers would be fighting the LTTE, or that the LTTE would prove to be such tough fighters. J.N. Dixit, then Indian high commissioner at Colombo (he became the national security adviser to Prime Minister Manmohan Singh in 2004), later recalled in his memoirs, 'Harkirat Singh told me that he envisaged IPKF's responsibility as a limited one, namely, the maintenance of law and order in Jaffna and Trincomalee as the Sri Lankan army and paramilitary forces had been withdrawn from those areas.'

When Dixit mentioned that the IPKF could have the additional responsibility of ensuring that the accord was implemented, Harkirat's response was: 'That is all very well, Sir, but I hope we do not get involved in a shooting match because of this Agreement.'

But this was precisely what came to pass. While trying to ensure that the Sri Lankan government and the LTTE adhered to the India–Sri Lanka accord, the IPKF soon found itself under pressure from both sides. Its delicate and difficult balancing act collapsed disastrously after the mass suicide of the LTTE prisoners, with the LTTE announcing its withdrawal from the India–Sri Lanka accord. Prabhakaran and his men were now openly on a confrontational path with the IPKF. They started attacking Indian troops at various places in northern Sri Lanka. India had to change tack too, with a swiftness that was almost surreal given its past pro-Tamil approach. The day after the mass suicide, General K. Sundarji, the Indian army chief, launched Operation Pawan, to wrest control of Jaffna from the LTTE.

Over the next thirty months, many military units took part in Operation Pawan. The units that were inducted the earliest bore the biggest brunt. Sheonan's unit, 10 Para Commandos, was one such.

~

In 1987 the Indian army had only three para commando battalions – 1, 9 and 10 – and they comprised volunteers who were reputed to be the absolute best of the best in soldiering. Physically extremely fit, mentally robust and trained to operate on their own in small teams, these men in their distinctive maroon berets worn at a jaunty angle matched up with the best in the world and took immense professional pride in wearing the Balidan (Sacrifice) badge on their shirt.

Sheonan Singh, who retired as a major general, is a tall, broad-shouldered man, with a rather unusual background for a para commando. He graduated as an engineer from Roorkee University and joined the army as a sapper officer. Even though he was a topper in early military courses, his blunt, outspoken manner didn't endear him to many of his superiors in the engineer unit. He volunteered for the famously rigorous commando course, and was sent to Belgaum for it.

The five-week course entails jumping from high walls, walking on narrow platforms and beams, slithering down ropes from helicopters, endurance runs of up to 40 kilometres carrying an 18.5-kilo battle load and rifle, battle obstacle courses, rock climbing, rappelling, combat firing and confidence jumps. Commandos are also taught survival techniques – how to live off the land – which includes eating snakes. Once a commando has killed and eaten a snake, the logic goes, he will not shy away from anything.

Sheonan topped the course at Belgaum and was subsequently posted as an instructor there. Two years later he volunteered to join 10 Para Commandos, which was stationed at Jodhpur.

In July 1987, he had just arrived at Jodhpur. He was

still on leave, settling his family in before formally joining duty, when he got orders late one night: he was to bring 10 Para Commandos to the airfield from where they would be flown to an unknown location. His commanding officer, Lt Col Dalbir Singh, had earlier been summoned to army headquarters at Delhi, and he too was to join the unit at the airfield.

Collecting 254 out of the 560 people in the unit – the rest were on summer leave – Sheonan boarded the aircraft. Dalbir Singh soon joined them, and only when the plane was airborne was the aircrew told that their destination was Sulur in Tamil Nadu. But their final destination was, in fact, Sri Lanka.

Soon after the para commandos landed at Sulur, a team of twenty men under Dalbir Singh left for Colombo to secure the Indian high commission there. Their main job was to move the Sri Lankan president, in case of a coup, to the safe premises of the Indian high commission. A second team of 110 para commandos went to Palali in northern Sri Lanka. In the event of a crisis, the second team would be flown to Colombo in helicopters provided by the IAF to support the first team, at the high commission. Sheonan was part of the third and last group of 110 para commandos, who were also moved to Palali: their task would be to capture Colombo airport in the event of a coup or other crisis.

Indian army HQ in Delhi had planned for various contingencies in Sri Lanka, mostly in anticipation of an attempt to overthrow the Sri Lankan President. Unfortunately, what they never planned for was the LTTE turning on its Indian masters.

~

Both the para commando teams based in Palali had their 'door loads' packed for a few days of fighting, ready to move the moment they got the go-ahead. A door load is a packet of arms, ammunition and other equipment needed during a battle, fitted with a beacon on top which starts blinking the moment the packet hits the ground. This 'door load' is thrown from the aircraft or helicopter before the para commandos move out.

Sheonan and his team settled into Palali, a hamlet on the outskirts of Jaffna. Palali was an important military airport, built by the British during the Second World War, and the main lifeline for the Jaffna peninsula. A high-security zone spread over 25 square kilometres around the airfield was the headquarters of the IPKF and the nerve centre of all Indian military operations in the country.

Every detail of Sheonan's time in Jaffna is still sharply etched in his mind, even though the events he was recalling had taken place nearly thirty years earlier. Most of the other military men involved in what had turned out to be an appalling military fiasco did not want to speak about it. As one former para commando said, 'I have forgotten and moved on. I have no wish to refresh my memory of those days.'

Para commandos, by the very nature of their training and role, are always on the alert for sudden emergencies. But, says Sheonan, a man of strong opinions which he doesn't hesitate to express, the rest of the army was not mentally prepared for fighting. 'General Harkirat Singh saw the IPKF as an extension of the peace station at Secunderabad. If left to him, he would have organized family welfare meets there.' Harkirat Singh turned out to be both unprepared for the task of confronting the LTTE and unwilling to adapt quickly to the fast-changing situation.

Shortly after Operation Pawan was launched, General Sundarji announced in Colombo that the Indian army would finish the LTTE in a week. On 6 October, the day Operation Pawan was launched, the LTTE's printing presses at Jaffna were destroyed by the Maratha battalion, and clashes between the LTTE and IPKF started at various places. But this information was not shared with all the IPKF troops. Sheonan and his men at Palali were certainly not aware of it.

On 10 October, a party of para commandos left

Palali at around 5 p.m. – as part of its routine logistical duties – to collect food supplies from the ration point at Kankasanturai, three kilometres to the west. It was a ten-minute journey by road. When his men didn't return till 6.30 p.m., Sheonan walked up to the Division HQ and told them, 'Our Jonga and five men are missing and we want to go and check their whereabouts.'

'Thank God someone wants to go and check,' the Colonel GS replied. That is when Sheonan came to know that such mishaps had happened with other IPKF units as well – more than thirty soldiers went missing that day, but not many units were willing to go looking for their men. Sheonan led a patrol on foot but was unable to find either the men or their vehicle. The Jonga was recovered from inside a house two months later; the bodies of the five men were never found.

They were the first casualties suffered by 10 Para Commandos since the 1971 war.

~

With the LTTE declaring war on the IPKF, Harkirat Singh was now short of troops. He needed more forces. Army headquarters had already earmarked 72 Infantry Brigade at Gwalior – with three infantry battalions of around 800 men each, under Brigadier B.D. Mishra – as a quick reaction force for a contingency task in Sri Lanka. Mishra's brigade headquarters, along with two of his three battalions – 4/5 Gorkha Rifles (4/5 GR) and 13 Sikh Light Infantry (13 Sikh LI) – arrived in Palali by air at 10 a.m. on 11 October.

Soon after the Sikh LI landed, Sheonan and the Commanding Officer of 13 Sikh LI, Lt Col R.S. Sethi, were summoned for a briefing at the Division HQ. Sethi was totally unprepared for the orders he received that day. His battalion was to land at Jaffna University ground in a heliborne operation that night. The para commandos under Sheonan were to precede Sethi's men and secure the landing zone for them.

Official records show that Sethi made repeated requests for the operation to be postponed by at least twenty-four hours: due to some logistical problems only 250 of his 800 men had arrived in Palali and he had no information about the area in which he was to operate. Harkirat Singh also pleaded for a postponement but was told that 'it was not desirable'. In the event, Sethi and his men followed Tennyson's oft-quoted words: 'Theirs not to reason why, theirs but to do and die'.

During the briefing, Sheonan was ordered to 'take off at 1 a.m. on the 12th, go and secure a landing zone in Jaffna University grounds. 13 Sikh LI will follow and they will take over the place from you. You will then move on foot to Jaffna town, go to the bus stand (which is 6–7 km away), and embark on vehicles placed there. You will have hot meals at Palali in the morning.'

Every commando operation has an alternate task but the Colonel GS had not mentioned any. When Sheonan asked for one, he gave the para commandos the alternate task of raiding and destroying the LTTE headquarters in the university complex. This alternate task – expanded to include the capture of the top LTTE leadership – was later portrayed as the main task for which the heliborne operation was launched by the IPKF. The official version claims that 13 Sikh LI was to capture the LTTE's military HQ at Jaffna University, while the para commandos were to capture the LTTE's political HQ located there by dawn on 12 October 1987. Mishra with 4/5 Gurkha Rifles would link up with the Sikh LI battalion by road. If all went according to plan, Jaffna would be in IPKF hands by the end of the operation.

The Division HQ had not selected an alternative landing zone for the heliborne operation if for some reason the forces were unable to land at the original landing zone. When Sheonan pointed this out, the Colonel GS hastily – and randomly – selected on the map the only open patch of ground in the vicinity, around two kilometres north of the university ground.

Sethi was given a civil map of 1938 vintage and he

and his 100-odd Sikh LI troops had to depend on that to get their bearings of the area they were going to that night. Sheonan and his para commandos were not even given that map. But Sheonan had been in Palali for over two months and had driven around and been to the Jaffna University campus out of curiosity, so he was somewhat familiar with the area. Sheonan had also managed to get coloured photocopies of gridded military maps of Jaffna from the Sri Lankan army's Northern Command, whose officers he had befriended.

'There was no intelligence available during our briefing, either about the place or the strength and disposition of the enemy,' Sheonan recounts.

This is not surprising, considering the IPKF was operating under several handicaps. For one, it had never been in conflict with the LTTE until then – in fact, top IPKF generals had landed at Jaffna University ground to meet LTTE chief Prabhakaran just four days earlier in a last-ditch effort at a patch-up.

The IPKF had around 6000 military personnel deployed in the Jaffna peninsula then, though the number would have been closer to 10,000 if all the units were at full strength. Since troops were flown in to Sri Lanka at very short notice, some 40 per cent of the men were on leave, away on training courses or busy with other duties.

The IPKF also vastly underestimated the strength and

fighting capability of the LTTE – it assumed the strength of its cadre to be between 1500 and 2500, and did not rate the Tamil fighters very highly. The IPKF leadership believed the LTTE would simply disintegrate as the Indian infantry advanced on Jaffna, and even told senior Sri Lankan army officials that the operation to capture Jaffna would be concluded in three days.

As Harkirat Singh's successor at Palali, Lt Gen. S.C. Sardeshpande, noted in his memoirs, *Assignment Jaffna*, Sundarji's order to capture Jaffna 'came as a shock to the IPKF after four months of lavish honeymoon with the LTTE; the IPKF had a lot of apprehensions, reservations, doubts' and 'nobody had thought that LTTE would hit IPKF in the face with benumbing violence unleashed by deadly IEDs and vicious small arms fire in built-up areas and across lagoons'.

Sheonan was witness to a conversation between Sundarji and Harkirat Singh at Palali airport on 8 October. When the army chief asked Singh for the plan of operations, Harkirat Singh said he would induct a heliborne battalion at Jaffna, which would then join up with the Maratha battalion at Jaffna Fort, and the IPKF would then be in full control of the city.

'See you in Jaffna on the 12th,' said Sundarji breezily, as he shook hands with Harkirat Singh and boarded his flight.

As General Gerry H. de Silva of the Sri Lankan army, then Security Forces Commander of Jaffna, observes in his memoirs, *A Most Noble Profession*, Harkirat Singh and his senior staff were overconfident and dismissive of the LTTE. The LTTE in fact were well armed, with AK-47s, G3 rifles and machine guns, and they had an almost unending supply of well-trained and battle-hardened fighters. The Indian army, in contrast, had not fought a war since 1971.

~

The plan for the Jaffna landings was simple. The IAF had four Mi-8 helicopters based at Palali and all four were allocated for the operation. Each of these would do five sorties, ferrying twenty soldiers to the university ground on each sortie. With a flying time of only about four minutes from Palali airfield to Jaffna University, the multiple sorties were not seen as a problem.

Eighty para commandos – twenty in each of the four helicopters – would be dropped in the first of five waves. They would be followed by 40 para commandos and 40 infantry troops from the Sikh LI in the second wave. In the subsequent three waves only the Sikh LI troops, including Sethi, would be dropped.

Interestingly, in August and September these same

Mi-8 IAF helicopters had ferried the LTTE leaders around as they met their cadres and other personnel. In retrospect, it is clear that the LTTE had used this 'honeymoon period' to gather every bit of information on the IPKF, while the IPKF considered the LTTE a friend.

During an aerial reconnaissance on the afternoon of 11 October, the IPKF realized that the landing ground at Jaffna University could accommodate only two Mi-8s at a time. So, instead of keeping two helicopters hovering in the air while the first two unloaded the troops, the IAF decided that the second pair of helicopters would take off from Palali only after the first two had disembarked the men and started their return leg to Palali.

The Jaffna University area was like many other university campuses in South Asia, with a grid of straight, intersecting roads setting off administrative, academic and residential buildings. The oval-shaped sports ground, which had unusually little grass cover for the monsoon season, had a big, shady tree in the centre. It was bounded by a muddy running track, 400 metres long. On its northern edge was a three-storey medical college building; an administrative building hugged its southern edge. The Kokuvil railway station, on the railway line running from Jaffna to Kankasanturai (north to south), lay 150 metres to the west of the ground. Some trees and small huts dotted the eastern side of the ground.

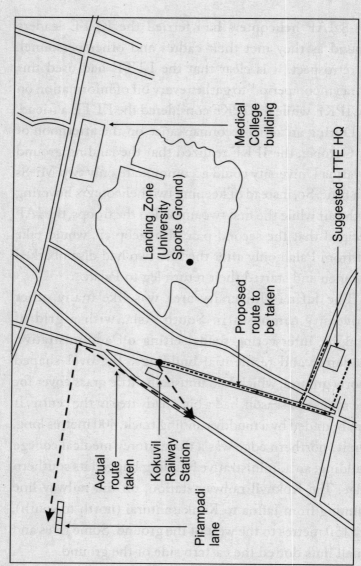

Medical College building

Suggested LTTE HQ

Landing Zone
(University Sports Ground)

Proposed
route to
be taken

Map of University Area

Actual
route taken

Kokuvil
Railway
Station

Pirampadi lane

Given the favourable meteorological forecast, the complete helicopter movement – ten waves of two helicopters each – was estimated to take about 90 minutes. The first two helicopters would take off at 0100 hours on 12 October. Certain that the possibility of ground fire was remote, the IPKF decided not to fit rocket pods to the Mi-8s to save weight.

The IPKF also asked the Sri Lanka Air Force (SLAF) to deploy one helicopter gunship in support of its mission. The SLAF was tasked to carry out a diversionary attack near the university during the landing operation, to overwhelm and distract the LTTE cadre.

So far, so good. There was no reason for the IPKF to be alarmed about anything.

~

After coming back from the reconnaissance helicopter flight on 11 October, Sheonan took stock of the situation. He decided to take with him the team of para commandos that had originally been assigned to secure Colombo airport in case of a political crisis. A total of 103 para commandos, including three officers, Sheonan, Major Rajiv Nair and Captain Ranbir Bhadauria, and the unit doctor, Captain Ajit Joseph Veniyoor, together with his nursing assistant, would land at the university ground with him. Veniyoor was physically the fittest of the para commandos, and very calm under pressure. As someone who could read and understand Tamil, he also acted as an intelligence officer for his comrades. Now a practising oncologist at Muscat, he says he has blotted out all memories of those fateful hours in Jaffna. On the other hand, Bhadauria, now living in retirement at Sitapur in Uttar Pradesh, where his wife works as an ophthalmologist, continues to be haunted by Jaffna and went back there in 2016 to try to exorcize painful memories.

While Sheonan gathered his team, Sethi, the Sikh LI CO, decided to nominate Major Birendra Singh as the leader of the Sikh LI team until Sethi landed. Birendra Singh was a relative of former union minister Natwar Singh, rated highly by his battalion and much loved by his men. Birendra Singh was to take over the landing zone from the para commandos, and Sethi and the rest of his unit would follow in the subsequent waves.

Then a tricky question arose. Sheonan asked Sethi who the commander of the joint team would be until Sethi reached – Birendra Singh or Sheonan? Sethi refused to put his men under Sheonan's command. Harkirat Singh dismissed it as a minor issue, but Sheonan felt it was important that this be settled as any decision taken by the commander – whether to abort the mission or to withdraw from the site – would have to be obeyed by the other person as a military order. Moreover, if Sheonan was the overall commander, he would wait till Sethi landed at the university to hand over the place to him. But the question was left unresolved.

Sheonan suggested to Sethi that he send more men with rifles in the initial sorties. Heavier stores like ammunition for bigger weapons could follow in the subsequent sorties. Sethi, who had just landed at Palali, said dismissively, 'Arrey, ye lungi wale kya kar lenge? [Come on, what can these lungi-clad LTTE chaps do?]'

At the para commando base, Rajiv Nair and Sheonan decided to take with them to Jaffna the two existing door loads that had been put together in preparation for a quick takeover of Colombo airport. The door loads had ammunition and stores to last for four days of intense fighting.

Briefing his men, Sheonan said, 'We may be landing in a fighting situation. Be prepared to land and fire. Each man should know the direction plan so that you don't end up shooting each other. Once you land, go as far as you can towards the edge of the field.'

Sethi and Birendra Singh attended Sheonan's briefing but did not take his words seriously. They thought that he was just trying to keep his team charged up and on high alert.

Sheonan then asked Major Anurag Nauriyal, the leader of the para commandos team assigned the heliborne task at the Indian high commission, to move to the Palali helipad with a high frequency (HF) wireless radio set. An HF radio set can communicate over unlimited distance, even across continents.

'Nauriyal at Palali helipad with an HF radio set was the only communication that we had with Palali. Division HQ had planned no communication, either then or later,' Sheonan says.

Sheonan, Bhadauria, Veniyoor and his nursing assistant would be in the first helicopter while Nair would be in the second one. Fifty para commandos were to go in the first wave of two Mi-8s to light up the landing zone for the following helicopters to land.

Everyone was excited. 'Finally, we were doing an operational task,' says Sheonan. Bhadauria recalls, 'We were a bunch of enthusiastic boys ready to become men under fire.'

~

The para commandos raised the battle cry 'Durge Bhawani ki Jai' as the two Mi-8s, piloted by Wing Commander Sapre and Squadron Leader Vinay Raj, took off on schedule at 1 a.m. on 12 October, carrying the first fifty men. Due to low drifting clouds and poor visibility, they could not adhere to the original briefing to fly at 300 metres altitude; instead, they flew at a lower altitude of around 200 metres.

The two helicopters observed a complete blackout – all lights were switched off, including the 'blade tracking' lights in the wing tips, which enable the pilots to manoeuvre in confined airspaces. The only visual cue for Vinay Raj to maintain the correct distance from Sapre's helicopter was the single formation light on top of the tail boom of the leading Mi-8. These formation lights were also switched off as the choppers entered the last few metres of their descent. In spite of the poor visibility, the two pilots managed to locate the landing ground. Sapre hovered 10 metres over the landing zone while the para commandos slithered down a rope to the ground. As he was alighting, Bhadauria's legs got entangled in the rope and he experienced some hair-raising moments as the helicopter took off with him dangling below it, desperately clutching the rope. Fortunately, the upward thrust of the helicopter untangled the rope in the nick of time and he jumped to the ground. It was the first of many lucky breaks for him over the next thirty-seven hours.

As they landed, Sheonan and his men immediately threw out the door loads. His men started running towards the edges of the ground to take their positions.

Sapre came out and gave a thumbs-up sign to Sheonan. The Mi-8s took off, and Sheonan realized that they were under fire from the LTTE. The sound of fire from the LTTE's Chinese-made AK-47s and German G3 rifles had been drowned by the noise of the helicopters. Sheonan looked at his watch. It was 1.20 a.m.

As the two Mi-8s took off using full power, they too came under fire from the LTTE though neither was hit. Intelligence reports later confirmed that the LTTE were broadly aware of the IPKF's plans – they had intercepted the IPKF's VHF radio transmissions – but not fully prepared for the first landing. Sapre radioed Palali to send in the second pair of Mi-8s. By then, Sheonan had spoken to Nauriyal at the Palali helipad on radio and told him that they were under fire. He also instructed Nauriyal not to pass on this information to the IAF pilots as they may hesitate to fly in more troops.

Immediately after landing, Sheonan was supposed to light up the landing zone with markers to allow the following helicopters to land. The T-shaped marking is done by lighting a set of 'goose lamps', which have a wick that burns for three to four hours. As soon as the para commandos lit the first goose lamp, the team came under heavy fire. Sheonan decided against lighting the lamps and informed Palali of the change of plans. As in many battles, the first casualty was the battle plan.

In a few minutes, the second set of helicopters with the rest of the para commandos was to arrive. Sheonan recalls that he and his men 'kept waiting and waiting but no choppers came'.

The second set of Mi-8s was piloted by Prakash and Duraiswami. When they approached Jaffna University, they noticed that the entire area was enveloped in the flashes of small arms fire and grenade blasts. Flashes of tracer bullets from the SLAF attack helicopter in the distance painted an even scarier picture in the darkness of night. The landing ground had also not been lit up. Prakash and Duraiswami failed to locate the landing ground and decided to abort the mission. They flew back to Palali with fifty-three para commandos still on board.

The official enquiry on the incident indicted Sheonan for not lighting up the landing zone as per plan. It remains controversial to date, with opinions divided over Sheonan's decision. There are those who believe that the second set of sorties would not have been aborted had the para commandos lit up the landing zone.

Sheonan had his reasons: 'I was the man on ground and took the call. If the landing zone had been lit up, the LTTE fighters would have brought more concentrated fire on fifty of us. Also, the next set of helicopters landing there would have been targeted with heavier and more effective concentrated fire.'

Meanwhile, both Sapre and Vinay Raj had landed back at Palali. Birendra Singh and twenty-nine soldiers of the Sikh LI boarded the Mi-8s and Sapre and Vinay Raj took off for Jaffna University again. By then, the LTTE had figured out that the helicopters were coming from the north. They waited with AK-47 assault rifles and machine guns on the top of the medical college building on the northern edge of the landing ground, covering the approach of the helicopters.

As Vinay Raj prepared for the second landing, he heard a sudden increase in the intensity of gunfire. He realized that it was not from ground-level fighting, but from atop the northern building, and aimed directly at him. His crew felt the helicopter taking hits, with distinctive thumps as 7.62mm rounds pierced the Mi-8's outer skin.

The Mi-8s landed, and the infantrymen disembarked from the rear and took lying positions on the ground as per standard training drill. Some of them moved behind bushes and started digging into the undulating ground for better cover from enemy fire. Unlike the para commandos, they did not attempt to move to the edges of the ground. They were already under fire, and a bullet pierced through the ANPRC-25 wireless radio set carried by Birendra Singh's radio operator. Birendra Singh was now without communication with his CO, Sethi.

Expecting the rest of his para commandos in the second lot of helicopters, Sheonan was surprised to see the infantrymen disembarking from them. He asked Sapre, 'Where are my guys?'

'I am under heavy fire, but don't worry, I will get your chaps,' Sapre assured him.

As Sheonan gave a thumbs-up sign to Sapre to take off, Sapre pointed to the heavy wooden crates lying inside the chopper. The Sikh LI troops had already dispersed, and Sheonan, his doctor, nursing assistant and the radio operator had no choice but to unload the crates themselves. Birendra Singh had come with 1.5 tonnes of ammunition for the mortars, which meant that only thirty men could fit in the two choppers. This ammunition would be needed only when the mortars came in the last sortie.

'I was irritated as hell. Firstly, at four of us unloading the whole stuff, but more so because I had specifically advised Lt Col Sethi to send more armed men in the first flight and he sent stores instead of soldiers,' Sheonan recounts.

The two helicopters took off again amid the thumps and thuds made by the gunfire hitting them. Compared to the earlier take-off, the higher intensity of gunfire could be distinctly felt by Sapre and Vinay Raj.

By then, the fifty para commandos had opened the two door loads and distributed all the ammunition among themselves. They were prepared for a long haul.

~

When Sapre and Vinay Raj landed back at Palali, they found out that Duraiswami and Prakash had returned without dropping their load of para commandos. Sapre had given his word to Sheonan, and he and Vinay Raj decided to do one more trip to drop the fifty-three para commandos.

On approaching the Jaffna University ground for the third time, both helicopters came under intense fire from the LTTE gun positions. The LTTE had now massed even greater firepower at the medical college building. As the two Mi-8s neared the ground, machine gun firing was coming thick and fast and the crew could feel the helicopters getting hit continuously. One burst from a G3 rifle went into the battery compartment just behind the cockpit section, while another bullet shattered the cockpit side windscreen of Vinay Raj's helicopter. Luckily the bullet missed the pilots and the crew. Another bullet entered the cockpit from the floor, passing exactly between the two pilots. The crew later counted seventeen bullet holes in the helicopter. The hydraulics system of

Sapre's Mi-8 was shattered by LTTE fire. The two pilots were, however, able to get the fifty-three para commandos to the Jaffna University ground.

As they were taking off, Sapre told Sheonan, 'I am afraid no more helicopters can come now.'

It was only Sapre's skill that ensured that his damaged helicopter got back to Palali. Neither of the Mi-8s could fly further missions. Sapre realized that the fury of the LTTE ground firing during the third run had been of higher intensity than the earlier ones. The next mission, if flown, would result in even greater damage than this one. The IAF decided to stop further sorties.

Sheonan learnt this from Nauriyal around thirty minutes after Sapre and Vinay Raj had taken off from the Jaffna University ground amid heavy firing. Only then, at 2.45 a.m., Sheonan claims, did the Division HQ – located barely 300 metres away from the helipad at Palali – realize that the soldiers were under heavy firing and that two helicopters were no longer fit to fly.

Sethi had marched up to the Division HQ, and was trying to justify why he had sent fewer men and more stores. When Harkirat Singh asked Singh about the weapons Birendra Singh's team was carrying, Sethi started with the most potent weapon his men were carrying, the medium machine gun. Weighing eleven kilos, an MMG is a belt-fed automatic weapon, supported on a tripod mounting, which fires a full-power 7.62mm rifle cartridge round. It fires 600–1000 bullets per minute.

'If there is an MMG, the lungiwalas dare not come near. These commandos keep on making unnecessary noise,' Harkirat Singh said. Meanwhile, Nauriyal told Sheonan to hold the LTTE at bay for some time, as the rest of the troops would come by foot. Even if they started immediately, it would take them at least three hours to cover the distance of 17 kilometres.

'If they were coming by foot now, why could we all not have come the same way? I had proposed that we all start at 9 p.m. and move cross-country, instead of using helicopters and telegraphing our intentions to LTTE. But that was shot down by the Division HQ,' Sheonan says now. The rationale for most decisions taken that day by the IPKF was understood, if at all, only by those who took them.

~

At the Jaffna University ground, firing from the LTTE had become intense. Para Commando Lok Ram, who came in the last Mi-8, later recounted to the *India Today* magazine, 'We thought everything was fine but as we were coming out of the helicopter we came under heavy fire from all sides. It was an impossible situation. We were fighting an enemy we could not even see.'

As is evident from a radio intercept the Sri Lankan army provided the IPKF later, the LTTE too had little hope of surviving the night: 'In a broadcast by Prabhakaran over the LTTE communication network on early night 11/12th October, it was stated that the LTTE command at the camp centre were unlikely to survive and their death appeared imminent. As such the LTTE fighters in this camp would die fighting to the last and may not come on the air again. Therefore, those who survive the offensive will move to other areas, goodbye to you, and the regional commanders should take charge of the operations.'

All in all, the Indian soldiers were lucky. The LTTE was not aware that there would be no more helicopter sorties that night. The bulk of their fighters remained at the top of the medical college building in anticipation of the next helicopter, hoping to bring it down. This meant that the LTTE were firing at the soldiers from a height, and unless someone 'had his name written on a bullet', the chances of getting hit were far fewer than if the LTTE had been firing from ground level.

Once Sheonan knew that no more soldiers were coming by helicopter, he asked the Division HQ (by then a radio connection had been established between HQ and

Sheonan) to spell out the orders for him. 'Leave Major Birendra there at the university ground with his men and proceed to destroy the LTTE headquarters. Then move to the bus station to come back to Palali,' he was told.

'I will take Major Birendra with me. Otherwise, come daylight, he will be killed here,' Sheonan suggested.

His suggestion was overruled. Even so, Sheonan asked Birendra Singh if, in spite of the order, he would like to come with the para commandos.

'No, I will wait for my battalion here. My CO will come. Else it will look as if I deserted them,' Birendra Singh replied.

Sheonan could not order the major as the Sikh LI troops were not placed under his command. He could only make suggestions, which Birendra Singh was free to accept or reject. Sheonan now says that had he been in charge, he 'would have never asked the Division HQ about the orders for Major Birendra and his men. I would have just taken them along with me.'

However, Sheonan was now following the orders to raid the LTTE headquarters, which had been the alternate task assigned to the para commandos. The Sikh LI troops were going to be on their own. As Birendra Singh's radio set had been shot through, Sheonan gave him a wireless radio set from one of the para commandos, who are authorized many more radio sets than an infantry battalion, so that he could stay in touch. That was the last Sheonan saw of Birendra Singh.

~

The LTTE headquarters was supposed to be a building on the southern side of the campus, on Tabbil Pedi Lane, a couple of roads behind the administrative building that abutted the southern edge of the sports ground.

By now it was clear to Sheonan that the administrative building was occupied by well-armed LTTE fighters. Unwilling to move through a built-up area, Sheonan decided to approach the LTTE headquarters by taking a detour towards the railway track that lay to the west of the sports ground, and he sent a patrol to check out the route.

Sheonan then took a headcount of his men and found he was one man short. The nursing assistant told Sheonan that the doctor was missing. 'I knew where he would be. I told the nursing assistant that he must have dozed off. We went back to the dugout where we had taken positions, and there he was, fast asleep, amidst all the firing! Doctor was that kind of character,' Sheonan recalls with a chuckle.

The patrol came back with an all-clear report for the route they would follow.

The para commandos moved stealthily towards their target. They had so far suffered no losses, and they had a firm plan of action.

It was now 3.45 a.m. The darkness of night was slowly giving way to the first signs of dawn. Barely had the para commandos moved 150 metres when they came under heavy fire from Kokuvil railway station. They responded by firing five rounds from their Karl Gustav rocket launchers, a weapon used mainly against tanks.

Through his night vision device, Sheonan could see a big group of LTTE fighters moving from the railway station towards the road the para commandos were supposed to take. The firing became intense. In trying to take cover, the para commandos crossed the railway line and spotted a single-storey house with a boundary wall and a small iron gate a few yards to the west of the railway station.

The house had a sloping roof of clay tiles popular in that area. They knocked on the door, which was opened by a middle-aged man. Communicating in a mixture of Tamil and broken English, he told Sheonan he was a professor at the local polytechnic. He said the LTTE leadership did not stay the night in the building he was planning to attack, but functioned from there only during the day. At night, Prabhakaran and others slept in a house a couple of hundred yards away. The old man cautioned Sheonan: the para commandos would easily be outnumbered by the 100–150 LTTE fighters that guarded Prabhakaran at any given time, he said.

Dismissing his advice, Sheonan decided to head to the house Prabhakaran was said to be sleeping in. But they didn't trust the professor. He was asked to suggest three routes, and the para commandos picked one – if he was leading them into a trap where the LTTE had laid an ambush, Sheonan reasoned, he would have insisted on one route. Sheonan then told the professor to guide them to the house. To make doubly sure that they were not walking into a trap, Nair put an additional condition. In his broken Tamil, he told the professor that his son-in-law would be walking with them as a hostage, with a para commando pointing his loaded rifle at the back of his head. If they came under fire, the son-in-law would be shot dead.

As soon as they left the professor's house, the para commandos came under fire from three directions, and the leading commando was hit. Immediately, the para commando with the rifle pointed to the son-in-law's head pressed the trigger. The professor's son-in-law died instantly.

Sheonan says that Nair's aim was only to threaten the professor but the para commando took the order literally. 'We felt very bad about it,' he says. 'We didn't believe the professor deliberately misled us. But such things happen in the heat of battle.'

Bhadauria noticed that a para commando had been shot in the thigh and was writhing in pain. He identified the hut from which the firing had come, 70 metres behind them, and ordered his rocket launcher team to target it. As three rounds hit the hut, the firing stopped, but the wails and screams of the women and children inside could be heard.

Although the professor had pointed them towards one house, the para commandos were now being fired upon from a group of houses. Intelligence reports later revealed that Prabhakaran used to sleep in a different house every night. That night, he had moved out of the Kokuvil East area at 4.15 a.m., when the first rounds were fired on the para commandos from the Kokuvil railway station.

But Sheonan didn't know it then. The intense firing continued as they made their way to Pirampadi Lane, about 500 metres from the professor's house. This was a pleasant neighbourhood, with houses lining both sides of the twenty-foot lane. As they entered the lane Sheonan and Bhadauria came under fire from a house 20 metres ahead. Their sten machine carbines firing, they charged towards the door of the house. A man came out of the house and rushed towards them, and when he was barely three feet away, in a reflex action, Sheonan fired and hit him on the chest. Both men's uniforms were splattered with his blood. It was only then that they realized that the man was unarmed. But now the other para commandos had entered the house and shot dead every man and woman inside.

What happened thereafter has given Bhadauria many sleepless nights. 'In the kitchen I saw a woman with her two-year-old boy clutching her sari. As though by reflex, my weapon opened up and the woman slumped to the ground. But I could not fire at that kid,' Bhadauria recounts. 'I had a little son at home, who was the same age. Then I told myself this child will grow up to be a terrorist, perhaps a suicide bomber. So I turned to my buddy Arvind, an Adivasi from Bihar – his rifle opened up and the little boy was silenced forever. It is a decision I will regret all my life. Everyone in that house was either an LTTE militant or their active supporter, but not that frightened little boy…'

The para commandos now stormed into six neighbouring houses on either side of Pirampadi Lane and took up positions there. These were mostly pucca houses, single-storey, with sloping tiled roofs, similar to the polytechnic professor's house. Sheonan gathered the family members of each house into one room in their respective houses. He chose rooms that did not face the road, and told the families to take their rations with them. The families were not to venture out of that room, unless instructed by the para commandos. 'By night, either we will all leave or we will all be dead,' Sheonan told them.

The LTTE fighters were holed up inside other houses in the area. The para commandos were under siege, caught in a hail of bullets from the surrounding houses.

This was the first time in his life that Sheonan had come under effective fire. Quickly assessing the situation, he distributed his men among the houses they were occupying. Sheonan and the doctor stayed in the central building where a medical post was set up to treat the wounded. Nair and Bhadauria were sent to the houses on the two extremities. With greater situational awareness and the advantage of daylight, the para commandos took up positions at the windows and ventilators of the houses, and started returning fire. Sheonan looked at his watch. It was now 6.20 a.m.

Three things were uppermost in Sheonan's mind: 'First, protect my chaps – I didn't want to lose any men. Second, fulfil the operational task of destroying the LTTE headquarters. And third, avoid killing any more civilians while doing this.'

By 5.30 a.m., Sheonan's CO, Dalbir Singh, who had been at the Indian high commission in Colombo, had flown to Palali, determined to join his unit which was in the thick of battle. The firefight between the 103 para commandos and the LTTE fighters was relentless. The morning sun had given way to dark clouds which threatened heavy showers, but the two sides seemed undeterred. Sheonan saw young men come on bicycles, join the LTTE fighters, take positions, join the firefight and then go back. He estimated that they were surrounded by 450 to 500 LTTE fighters, a number confirmed by intelligence reports later.

The para commandos suffered their first casualties within an hour: three of them were hit by bursts from LTTE fighters. One of them, receiving three bullets on his chest, died instantly. The other two succumbed to their injuries a few hours later. Through the ventilator, Sheonan shot dead the man who had got the three para commandos. Then he ran through a hail of bullets to pick up the dead fighter's G3 rifle from the lane. He discarded his highly unreliable Sten carbine and started firing with the German-made rifle as it used the same 7.62mm ammunition used in the Indian rifles.

As the para commandos had brought the surplus ammunition of two door loads with them, they didn't have to worry about conserving ammunition.

The threatened downpour did not come, and the firing continued. Bhadauria, in the last house in Pirampadi Lane, had a lucky escape when a bullet hit the chair he had vacated just a second earlier. Later, spotting a group of LTTE fighters in an open space between two houses in the lane, Bhadauria and his men let loose a barrage of fire, and killed twelve of them.

~

Meanwhile, what was happening with Birendra Singh and his men?

Till around 10.30 a.m., the para commandos could hear the sound of firing from the Jaffna University ground, particularly of the MMG being fired by the Sikh LI. Suddenly, the MMG stopped firing – and then the sound of MMG firing appeared closer. This was ominous – it could mean only one thing. Sheonan's next radio message to Palali base relayed the tragedy in a short, terse sentence: 'The MMG from the university ground is now firing at us. Major Birendra and all his men are dead.'

As Sheonan had feared when he left Birendra Singh behind, the infantrymen had been overwhelmed by LTTE firing after dawn broke: picked off by LTTE snipers, twenty-seven of them, including Birendra Singh, had been killed and only three were alive. These three decided that their best chance of survival was to launch an assault and recapture the MMG lost to the LTTE. So, giving their remaining ammunition to Sepoy Gora Singh, who would provide covering fire with his rifle, two of them led a bayonet charge on the LTTE men holding the MMG. This was like a throwback to battles fought a century ago, when soldiers, having expended their ammunition, fixed their bayonets to their rifles and charged the enemy in a final act of desperation.

The two men were shot and Sepoy Gora Singh was captured alive by the LTTE – probably because the LTTE were keen to learn from him how to operate weapons such as the rocket launcher they had captured from the IPKF in the past few days. (Gora Singh was released in November 1988 in an exchange of prisoners between the LTTE and the IPKF, and continued to serve in the 13 Sikh LI.)

The Sri Lankan army, which had constantly been monitoring both the IPKF and the LTTE radio networks, had a pretty good idea of how Birendra Singh and his infantrymen, as well as Sheonan and his para commandos, were faring. In its assessment of the tragedy, it concluded that the infantrymen had been airdropped without proper briefing about the terrain they would land in, or warning about the LTTE's firepower and tactics. The Indian army's official report, though it acknowledges that Birendra Singh's men 'put up a gallant fight for hours unmindful of LTTE demand to surrender', blames them as they 'did not prepare the defences during the night and therefore, on 12 October at dawn, came under accurate fire from the buildings dominating the LZ [landing zone] area'. The title of the paragraph in this report says it all: The Disaster.

~

The fierce gunfight between the LTTE and Sheonan and his men continued in Pirampadi Lane. The two sides were separated by barely 40 metres at places, and not a minute passed without at least three or four bursts of AK-47 or G3 fire being heard. While the LTTE were able to move in and out of the area, the para commandos were pinned down inside the houses.

Every hour, a group of fifteen to twenty LTTE fighters would try to storm one of the houses. Dressed in their lungis, they would assault the house from three sides, firing and shouting at the top of their voices. Bhadauria had beaten back one such assault, as had the other para commandos, but Sheonan realized around 10 a.m. that more effective firepower was needed. He decided to call for artillery fire to target the houses from which the LTTE were firing on his men.

An artillery gun can be fired from kilometres away. The person firing doesn't see the target, but calculates the path and the trajectory of the shell based on the position of the target on a map. When the first shell lands, someone present close to the target gives 'corrections' for the subsequent firing – say, 50 metres north, 100 metres east and so on. Depending on the type of artillery gun, a target in a range of up to 35 kilometres can be aimed at.

Sheonan knew that 54 Artillery Brigade was at Palali, with its guns. But as soon as he requested for artillery fire, he received a shock: the artillery brigade had brought the guns to Sri Lanka but not the ammunition for it.

Sheonan looks shocked and incredulous as he recalls, 'Even when we go for exercises, we carry training ammunition so that soldiers are comfortable handling live ammunition. Here we were, deployed overseas, and there was no artillery ammunition whatsoever.'

Fortunately, the Sri Lankan army came to the rescue. They had three tubes of 120mm mortars at Jaffna Fort. A mortar is a smaller version of the artillery gun but it is not on wheels and has a shorter range. A crew from the Sri Lankan army engineers was manning these mortars.

But one problem remained. There were no common gridded military maps available with the IPKF's Division HQ, the Sri Lankan army mortar detachment and

Sheonan to guide the mortar fire to the correct spot. So Division HQ decided to send Major Chaudhary, an army pilot, in his Chetak helicopter, with a map, to hover over Sheonan's location and pass on the information to the Sri Lankans. However, Chaudhary didn't know exactly where the para commandos were.

Sheonan decided to indicate his location by using the most primitive method: fire and smoke. Taking a sari from the family, Sheonan's team doused it in kerosene, set it alight and put it on a stick atop the roof of the house occupied by them. Chaudhary saw the fire, and with his helicopter hovering over the house started talking to Sheonan using his radio set.

To give 'correction', Sheonan sent two of his para commandos to the roof of the house. It was going to be a three-way communication: para commandos on the roof to Sheonan, Sheonan inside the house to Chaudhary in the helicopter and, Chaudhary to the Sri Lankan army at Jaffna Fort, with all the attendant dangers of the message getting distorted – as in a game of Chinese whispers.

A Sri Lankan soldier fired the mortars, and the first round fell some distance away from the target. Based on the distances judged by the two para commandos on the roof, Sheonan relayed the corrections: 100 metres north and 50 metres east. The maps were not needed any more. The rounds were landing closer to the target. As Chaudhary's helicopter was running low on fuel, he returned to Palali. So Sheonan started directly communicating via his radio set with the Sri Lankan soldiers. And then he gave this one 'correction'.

'I didn't know that I could give a correction of up to 25 metres for the mortar. I thought the minimum I could pass was in multiples of 50 metres,' Sheonan recounts. To get closer to the houses from which they were directly under fire, he passed a correction of 50 metres south. This turned out to be disastrous: the next shell landed at the buildings the para commandos were in.

Gangaram, a para commando positioned on the roof to judge the accuracy of the falling shells, lost his right leg as the shell fell. Havaldar Devi Singh, his detachment commander, ran towards him but before he could reach him Gangaram put the barrel of his rifle to his own chest, and pressed the trigger.

The same shell also sliced off the hip of Umesh, Sheonan's helper. The doctor asked Sheonan whether he should try to save the heavily bleeding Umesh, which would entail the use of much of the bandage and medicine supplies, leaving hardly anything for further casualties.

'Don't ask me. Take a practical decision, take a medical call. If the choice is between saving one life or saving ten lives, we must save ten lives,' Sheonan told the doctor. The doctor made his choice. He used the saris and lungis available in the house as dressing to plug the bleeding but to no avail. Umesh was in great pain. He died two hours later. Sheonan doesn't wear his emotions on his sleeve, nor is he given to self-doubt or regretful reflection. Looking back on what must have been a traumatic experience – his mistake leading to the death of two of his men – he says in his typically laconic way: 'When you are in the thick of operations, casualties don't affect you. The incident hit me two days later. And I felt bad about the mistake in directing the mortar. My regret was that had I been trained to take an "artillery shoot", I would have known about the 25 metres correction.'

The mortar shelling, though it had cost two lives among the para commandos, had done its job. At around 11 a.m., the LTTE called up the Division HQ at Palali asking for the mortar shelling to be stopped as they had lost forty men and wanted to evacuate their casualties. Two mortar shells had landed on target. The Division HQ informed Sheonan of this communication.

With three of his men dead, Sheonan was in no mood to negotiate with the enemy, and called for more mortar fire from the Sri Lankan army. But the Sri Lankan soldier told him that he had only three rounds left on each of the three mortar tubes. Sheonan asked the Division HQ if they had mortar ammunition which could be given to the Sri Lankans. Division HQ replied it had not brought any mortar ammunition either from India. Sheonan chose to keep the nine rounds with the Sri Lankan army as a reserve for an emergency.

The LTTE fighters were no longer being targeted by mortar fire, and the firefight between the para commandos and the LTTE continued. By 3 p.m., Sheonan had reorganized his team, and now they were occupying only five houses. To bring his men out of the sixth house, he ran through heavy fire from the LTTE, and once again emerged miraculously unscathed.

Sheonan had yet another lucky escape shortly afterwards. Standing behind Para Commando Manohar, who was firing with his rifle through a window, he had just turned around to exit the room when a 40mm grenade hit the wall behind him. His back and neck were full of splinters and pellets, which came to light only when he went to the doctor with a high fever a few days later. Most of the splinters were too close to his backbone and remain there to this day. But Manohar died a few minutes later, at the same spot, when a bullet went through his mouth and his head.

Having lost many men in their attempts to capture the houses occupied by the para commandos, the LTTE stopped their assault at around 4 p.m. except for stray firing now and then. But a freak accident turned the day even more nightmarish for Sheonan and his men, still holed up in those five houses on Pirampadi Lane.

As a para commando fired his rocket launcher – which is normally fired in an open area – from a window in one of the houses the back-blast brought down the partition wall behind him and the roof of one room caved in. This was where the residents of that house had been told to take shelter. All seven members of the family died instantly.

Across the lane, at the centre of the buildings from where the LTTE were firing, a lone hut prominently stood out from the rest of the pucca houses. Although no one had fired from there, Sheonan's men were keen to destroy the hut as it presented an easy target, but he stopped them. 'We might need that hut at night to indicate our location to someone. We can set it alight then,' he told his men. He turned out to be prescient.

As the evening gave way to night and the skies opened up, the LTTE's lack of night-fighting capability became obvious. If Sheonan and his men had to get out, they needed to escape then, under the cover of darkness. They, however, had a problem: six men dead and fourteen wounded. Sheonan told Palali base that it was not possible for them to fight their way back to Palali with all their dead and wounded comrades – at best they could carry six of the wounded but the rest would have to be left behind, at the mercy of the LTTE. They needed help to bring back all the dead and wounded to Palali. Fortunately, that help was on its way.

~

Back at Palali, within hours of launching the operation, the Division HQ was in a state of panic. Harkirat Singh, a hero of the 1971 war, had already pulled out everything he had under his command to salvage the situation. When the helicopter sorties had to be abandoned, Mishra's 72 Infantry Brigade had been told to move on foot towards Jaffna University. This advance was led by 4/5 GR. The rest of the brigade was still at Palali, waiting for some more men to fetch up.

Later that morning, Harkirat Singh took off in the Chetak helicopter for a reconnaissance of the Jaffna University area. He was barely airborne when a machine gun round fired by the LTTE went through the three-inch space between the seats of the general and his pilot. The helicopter returned to Palali.

Harkirat Singh now modified his plans. Sethi – who still had no information about his twenty-nine soldiers under Birendra Singh, and with his two companies yet to land in Sri Lanka – was to advance with eighty of his men towards Jaffna in six vehicles and link up with 4/5

GR. Sethi started his advance at 6.30 a.m. on the 12th, with his troops coming under intermittent fire from the LTTE – and linked up with 4/5 GR on the outskirts of Urelu village six kilometres short of Jaffna. He could not move any further towards Jaffna because of a siege laid by LTTE fighters.

Sethi was now ordered to take a detour and march cross-country to link up with Birendra Singh and his men. Sethi felt duty-bound to make every effort to save the lives of as many of his men as he could. But he was let down by the Division HQ. Sethi was misled into believing that Birendra Singh and his men had been trapped because the helicopter pilots had dropped them at the alternate landing zone – an open patch of land randomly selected off the map by the Division HQ when Sheonan had asked for one.

The truth emerged later during the enquiry. The alternate landing zone was too small to accommodate even a Chetak helicopter, let alone two Mi-8s. Either because of confusion about the battle plan or because it wanted to cover up the fact that it had ordered the para commandos to leave the Sikh LI behind at the Jaffna football field, the Division HQ tried to claim that these men had been killed because the IAF had dropped them at the alternate landing zone, while the para commandos were waiting for them at the university ground.

This misinformation continued to be widely reported even later in the media. On 21 October 1987 *The Hindu* reported: 'Unfortunately in the darkness, the Sikh LI jawans were put down in a clear ground some 2 km away from the intended Landing Zone. The Para Commandos disembarked successfully but the Sikh LI jawans were trapped in a heavily built up area, and though surrounded fought valiantly for 24 hours before being overwhelmed.'

The same details were repeated in a story in *India Today* in February 1988.

Believing that Birendra Singh was trapped in the alternate landing zone, Sethi started moving towards that open patch – with no local guides or proper maps, in a heavy downpour and under firing from the LTTE fighters. Having taken a detour from Urelu village they now reached Kondavil, a kilometre short of the alternate landing zone, but found they could not go beyond it. The LTTE had taken strong positions there, and Sethi's troops came under heavy fire. He lost five jawans, and another twenty-seven were injured.

Havaldar Kuldeep Singh, who was badly wounded during that action, later told *India Today*: 'We were pinned down by snipers firing at us from all sides. Five men from our unit died. It was very difficult. We have not been trained for this kind of battle.'

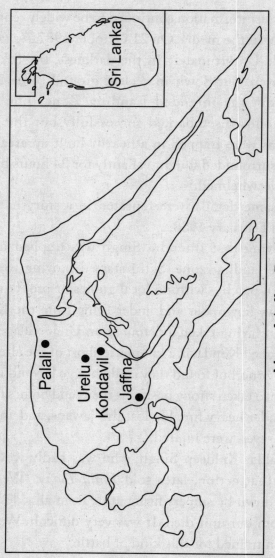

Map of Jaffna Peninsula

Everything that could go wrong had gone wrong. Harkirat Singh came to know later that the LTTE had intercepted the IPKF's radio communication network and were always a step ahead of the Indian soldiers and had enough time to plan an ambush.

The situation at 6 p.m. on 12 October was: Birendra Singh and twenty-nine men of the Sikh LI battalion at Jaffna University ground either missing or dead; Sheonan and his 102 para commandos (no one at HQ then knew that six of them were dead) surrounded by 500 LTTE fighters at Kokuvil East; Sethi with his Sikh LI column on their mission to rescue Birendra Singh and his men trapped by the LTTE at Kondavil; and 4/5 GR blocked by the LTTE and unable to move beyond Urelu temple crossing.

~

In the meantime, the rest of Sethi's Sikh LI battalion had landed at Palali from India. They, along with the tanks from 65 Armoured Regiment which had landed at 8.30 a.m., were ordered to join Mishra's 72 Infantry Brigade. Sheonan's CO, Dalbir Singh, insisted on joining the tanks and the freshly arrived Sikh LI troops. Mishra was now tasked by Harkirat Singh to rescue Sethi and his men held up at Kondavil and the 10 Para Commando men fighting the LTTE fighters in Kokuvil.

The commander of the tank troops was Major Anil Kaul. He had landed at Palali with two of his tanks and was surprised when he heard a despondent Harkirat Singh exclaim in Punjabi: 'I was sent to keep the peace. Suddenly they expect me to fight a war.' At the Division HQ, the short briefing he got from the Colonel GS left him perplexed. He was told that 'the road to Jaffna had been cleared of all opposition – however, I was to be careful of improvised explosive devices, snipers sitting on trees or high buildings along the road, and medium machine guns operating from hides. Otherwise, the road was clear.' Kaul didn't quite know what to make of this briefing which said two conflicting things. He was further instructed: 'Assist 72 Infantry Brigade for the establishment of a firm base for the capture of the LTTE HQ in Jaffna University.'

'At 10.30 a.m. we exited Palali base with a company of infantry riding piggyback on my tanks, and TV cameras of Doordarshan capturing on film a scene which was repeatedly played on TV screens back home, so as to give the impression of the advent of a large body of tanks and troops in the battle for Jaffna,' Kaul later recounted.

In an hour, he had reached the Urelu temple crossing and joined up with Mishra's brigade, which had reached the officers of 4/5 GR sheltering in a depression in the road. Dalbir Singh and Kaul were sent to Kondavil where Sethi and his men were stranded. They brought them back to the Urelu temple crossing by 8.30 p.m., coming under fire in the process. Dalbir Singh, who was riding on Kaul's tank, recalls that when he admitted he was scared, the para commando havaldar with him laughed and said, '*Sahab, agar yahaan goliyan nahin chalengi toh kya phool barsenge?* [Sir, if not bullets what do you expect here – a rain of flowers?]' A shamed Dalbir Singh quickly recovered his nerve. The bullets that day didn't have his name on them, but Kaul was not so lucky. He was severely wounded. While his tank was passing through narrow lanes and he had momentarily opened his tank's cupola door, a 40mm grenade fired by the LTTE hit the turret. The explosion severed his finger, while splinters hit him in the eye and arm. His men put him on morphine and kept him at Mishra's location at Urelu.

The task of bringing out Sheonan and his men from Pirampadi Lane, five kilometres away, was still pending.

~

It was then decided that Dalbir Singh, along with some troops of Sikh LI, would go along with these tanks to bring back Sheonan and his men. Dalbir Singh and two of his para commandos sat atop the three – a third tank, stationed at Palali, had also been deployed – Soviet-made T-72 tanks and started moving.

Dalbir Singh had flown over the area often in the past two months and was familiar with the layout of its roads and railway lines. In what he now calls 'a moment of divine inspiration', he decided to move the tanks along the Palali–Jaffna railway line which passed to the left of Jaffna University. 'If I had not followed the railway track I would never have reached my men,' says Dalbir. The LTTE, who were waiting to ambush them on the roads and lanes, were taken by surprise. The railway track did not have heavy embankments and so the tanks could move smoothly.

It was well past midnight when Dalbir Singh asked Sheonan for his exact location. Giving exact directions in an unknown area was a futile exercise, so Sheonan ordered his men to set that single hut on fire. 'We have put a hut on fire. Climb a tree and you will see the fire. To get to the hut, you will hit a major road crossing and then take a right,' Sheonan told his CO.

Dalbir Singh found his way around without much difficulty. By 4 a.m. on 13 October, Sheonan had taken stock of his men and material and reported to his CO: six para commandos dead – three in the initial firefight, two in shelling and one shot by the window in the evening – and fourteen wounded.

This is one record Sheonan is proud of. 'More than twenty-six hours of intense fighting, with no artillery support, and we were able to keep our casualties to a minimum. Compare this to what others suffered during the same period,' he says.

Now that they had the tanks with them, Dalbir Singh and Sheonan decided to blow up the houses from where the LTTE fighters were firing. But one tank had finished all its ammunition en route, the other had a round stuck in its barrel and the third tank didn't have a gunner in the crew who could fire. They asked a gunner from the second tank to fire the gun of the third tank but he just couldn't use the gun. It took him forty-five minutes to fire one shot from the tank, leaving both Dalbir Singh and Sheonan demoralized.

Worried about impending daybreak they decided to quickly make their way out while they still had the cover of darkness. But then the seniormost JCO with the tanks reported that one of his tanks had got bogged down in a slushy area, and they needed a recovery vehicle to pull it out from there. At the end of his tether by then, Sheonan resorted to some colourful language to tell the JCO that they would leave him behind with the tank, and the LTTE would next morning teach him everything about how to pull out his tank using his private parts.

Jolted into action, the JCO threw out the driver of the tank, took his seat and reversed the tank with such ferocity over a small house that the house was completely destroyed (fortunately, the house was empty). The para commandos loaded their six dead and fourteen injured comrades on top of the tanks, as they started their journey back to Palali. They wanted to travel the maximum distance before dawn.

The Sikh LI soldiers who had accompanied Dalbir Singh had been on the move from Gwalior to Agra to Palali to Kokuvil, all in the last forty-eight hours, and were so exhausted that most of them just dozed off as soon as they reached Sheonan and his para commandos. They were woken up and told to move.

As they were about to leave, one of Sheonan's JCOs told Dalbir Singh that he wanted to show him something. He took his CO into the house he had been deployed in during the day and opened an almirah. The almirah was stacked to the top with cash and gold.

'We have not even touched it. Tomorrow someone might allege something against us and so I wanted to show it to you,' the JCO said. The CO called the house owners and asked them to verify that all their valuables and money were intact. They repeated the exercise with the owners of every single house, till all of them were satisfied that the Indian soldiers had taken nothing.

'Death was so close that day,' Sheonan reflects, 'that if anyone was tempted to do something wrong – and they had ample chance to do it – he wouldn't do it.'

In her book *Broken Palmyrah*, the human rights activist and Jaffna University professor Dr Rajani Thiranagam – who was later killed by the LTTE – makes special mention of the para commandos, when she writes about human rights violations by the Sri Lankan army, IPKF, LTTE and other Tamil groups during 1987–88. She says a 'grey haired Major' of the commandos – Sheonan – treated the families at Kokuvil East with dignity, showed concern for civilian lives and ensured that nothing was looted from the houses.

～

Daylight had broken on 13 October by the time the tanks, accompanied by Dalbir Singh and his men, reached the railway line, a kilometre away. As the para commandos walked alongside the tanks, they were fired on from houses on both sides of the railway line. As none of the tanks were in a position to use their main guns, they mounted an MMG on top of each of the three tanks. A Sikh LI soldier manning the MMG got a burst from an AK-47 on his chest and died. So a wounded para commando on top of the tank started manning that MMG.

The tanks were now making a bad situation worse. The barrel of a tank brought down an electric pole and got entangled in the electric cable. The tank dragged the cable and the pole for a few hundred metres, and disentangling it took a precious twenty minutes while LTTE fighters kept up heavy firing. The soldiers were lucky to make their way through it.

It was 7 a.m. when they reached Mishra at the Urelu temple crossing. Mishra, who had taught Sheonan at Staff College, greeted him with a cheerful hello.

Sheonan's reply was blunt and clear: 'Forget the hello, sir. We must get out of here immediately or we must start digging down. They are following us and they will be here very soon.'

For a moment Mishra didn't get what Sheonan was saying. The men and officers were all sitting calmly in groups in that open patch of ground, least expecting an attack. But Mishra quickly issued orders that they would all return to Palali: 13 Sikh LI would lead the move, followed by 10 Para Commandos, and 4/5 GR would move on a separate axis along the railway line.

The Sikh LI soldiers, having taken the brunt of LTTE assaults since the previous night, were up and running in a jiffy. The para commandos followed, and Mishra joined Sheonan. But Mishra's radio operator was unable to connect him to the 4/5 GR CO, Lt Col I.B.S. Bawa. So Sheonan offered to run the 100 yards back to the battalion and pass on the message.

'I will go and tell them to move quickly. If they don't, they will be butchered,' Sheonan suggested.

'No, no, don't say butchered. Just tell them that commander has ordered that they move quickly,' Mishra replied.

On reaching the 4/5 GR location, the first person Sheonan encountered was the adjutant of the battalion, a young captain. Sheonan gave him the orders of the brigade commander, but the hassled young man was dismissive of Sheonan: 'You don't have to tell me what to do. I take my orders from my old man [i.e., the CO].'

His CO, Bawa, was barely 50 yards away. When Sheonan reached him and passed on Mishra's orders, the CO asked: 'Who are you? You f*** off. I am commanding my battalion.'

Sheonan was outraged: but he understood the CO's problem. The Gurkha battalion was unwilling to move because they had been pinned down by the intensity of LTTE fire. They should ideally have either moved earlier or prepared themselves to fight till the night, when they could have got out under the cover of darkness. But the men had neither deployed themselves to fire effectively nor dug their positions to take cover and fire. Moreover, the officers were not with their men but bunched in a single group near the railway line.

The whizz of AK-47 shots was getting closer. Sheonan dashed back to Mishra and told him that the battalion CO had refused to move. Mishra shrugged and said, 'No point trying to persuade them – the CO has been killed.' In the two minutes that Sheonan had taken to run back to Mishra after talking to Bawa, he had been shot by the LTTE (in fact Bawa, critically wounded, died a few hours later).

CO 4/5 GR had been especially targeted because of an LTTE tactic that the IPKF had not yet figured out. The LTTE snipers were adept at picking out officers from among a body of Indian soldiers, looking out for those who wore epaulettes with stars, who were shadowed by a radio operator and the distinctive headgear and battledress that were other giveaways of their rank. Picking up these cues, LTTE snipers killed a disproportionately large number of IPKF officers in the first few days.

Under the cover of three tanks – the LTTE fighters didn't know that the tank guns weren't working so they didn't come too close – Mishra, Dalbir Singh, Sheonan and the rest of the para commandos and the Sikh LI soldiers started walking towards Palali. As soon as they reached Pullampalai, a small IPKF administrative base, Harkirat Singh ordered the para commandos to go back and evacuate the gravely injured 4/5 GR CO. The para commandos felt they were in no shape to go back after what they had been through over the past two days, but they prepared to make the hazardous journey once again. It seemed their ordeal would never end.

Dalbir Singh prepared a team of twenty para commandos under Bhadauria to go back to the Urelu temple crossing. But once again they came under LTTE fire and they had to stop and take cover. By then, news came that apart from Bawa, 4/5 GR had lost two other officers, two JCOs and fifteen jawans, and another forty-two were injured. It was not possible for Bhadauria to evacuate all of them. He was asked to fall back to Pullampalai. At around 1 p.m., the Sri Lankan army sent its helicopter gunships to the Urelu temple crossing area and targeted the LTTE fighters. Only then were the tanks able to go and bring the dead and wounded 4/5 GR troops to the field hospital.

From Pullampalai, these tired men boarded military vehicles to return to Palali. Sheonan was driving the leading one-ton truck and Dalbir Singh was in the co-driver's seat. They had moved a kilometre when Sheonan saw three men on the road. He stopped the vehicle and fired on them. The men ran away. When his CO asked him why he had done so, Sheonan said that they were surely up to some mischief.

This convoy crossed the spot uneventfully, but three days later an IPKF tank was blown up at exactly the same place. The LTTE had buried barrels of explosives under the road and when Sheonan and Dalbir Singh spotted them, the three men had been trying to fix the final connection of the wires to detonate the explosives.

It was around 2 p.m. on 13 October that the para commandos reached Palali for a hot meal, a full thirty hours later than the original battle plan had estimated.

~

After this disastrous operation, Major General A.S. Kalkat took charge at Palali. Harkirat Singh was later moved out of Sri Lanka and so was Mishra. When Kalkat took charge, he asked the para commandos to go back and destroy the building overlooking the Jaffna University ground from where the helicopters had been attacked. That was to be by way of retribution, to convey a message to the LTTE.

But it was a medical college, and the para commandos resisted, saying that it would serve no purpose. Moreover, the three-storey concrete structure would need a lot of explosives to destroy it. So they were asked to destroy the LTTE HQ instead, the one Sheonan was supposed to destroy after landing at the Jaffna University ground on 12 October.

It was still the month of October and the rains hadn't let up. The para commandos walked from Palali to Kokuvil with a three-ton truck full of explosives to destroy that building. 'The weather was horrible. It was hot and sultry, with heavy rain. We were also being fired upon by the LTTE, and this order which put our lives in danger just to demolish an empty building made no sense,' says Sheonan.

A frustrated Sheonan started distributing sheets of paper to the para commandos, asking them how many of them would still volunteer to be a para commando. The para commando units are entirely drawn from volunteers. But that day, 90 per cent of the men wrote No.

Dalbir Singh admonished Sheonan: 'Why are you doing this?'

'Let's just have some good fun. If some of us have to die, so be it. But not for this idiotic job,' Sheonan replied. He laughed as he told me this story. That evening they destroyed the building.

As he was relating this, Sheonan's wife, Paramjit Kaur, entered the room. I asked her what she remembered most about the time her husband was deployed in Sri Lanka.

She recalled that after the battalion left for Sri Lanka, the wives of many para commandos came to her house and, in true Rajput tradition, hung their bangles in her living room. This was their way of saying that they trusted Sheonan to bring their husbands back alive. Sheonan interrupted her to say that that was the only time in their lives she ever wrote him a letter. Right after the Jaffna University landing disaster, he received a letter from her that said: 'We can live without you with honour. But we cannot live with you with dishonour. Just do your duty.'

Sheonan said every step he had taken had been guided by his determination to do his duty and do it with honour – and that included disregarding orders from Division HQ during the Jaffna operation. 'If I had taken their orders literally,' he said, 'I and all my men would have been killed.'

He added that he also had 'a family legacy to uphold', the legacy of his uncle Bhagat Singh. Hanged by the British at the age of twenty-three, Bhagat Singh was Sheonan's father Ranbir Singh's elder brother.

~

The ultimate accolade for Major Sheonan Singh and his men of 10 Para Commandos came from the LTTE.

During the exchange of prisoners on 18 November 1988 – when Sepoy Gora Singh of 13 Sikh LI, the only survivor from the Jaffna University ground, was returned – the LTTE's deputy leader Mahattaya told the IPKF that 'the commandos who landed at Kokuvil to raid the LTTE camp carried out the operation boldly and they were tough and brave soldiers'.

On his part, Sheonan too expressed admiration for his adversary. He told the army study group that arrived in Palali to prepare a report on IPKF operations, 'You still believe that these lungi-wearing Tamils know nothing about fighting. It doesn't matter what he is wearing, he is a far superior soldier to us.'

~

Lt Col Dalbir Singh, Sheonan and Sepoy Gangaram got Vir Chakras for the operation. Major Rajiv Nair and Captain Veniyoor were awarded Sena Medals for gallantry. Thanks to Major Sheonan's testimony at an Inter-Services Court of Inquiry into the Jaffna University operation which cleared their names, four of the IAF helicopter pilots were awarded Vir Chakras a year later, while the four co-pilots got Vayu Sena Medals for gallantry.

For Major Birendra Singh and the other twenty-eight men of 13 Sikh LI, slaughtered like sitting ducks in the Jaffna University ground, there were no coffins draped in the Indian tricolour, and no funerals with military honours – their bodies were never found. According to one persistent rumour they were cremated en masse by the LTTE; according to another they were all buried together in an unmarked grave.

~

The IPKF lost 1155 men in Sri Lanka between 1987 and 1990, when it withdrew from that country. Today, a black granite memorial near Palali airport stands as a sombre tribute to the IPKF men who died in that ill-fated operation in October 1987.

Although several of those who served in the IPKF have penned their memoirs, the defence ministry has not released the official history of Operation Pawan. The seventy men who fought and died at Jaffna during those thirty-seven hours from 12 to 13 October 1987 remain largely forgotten. They were part of a disastrous military misadventure that nobody wants to remember.

Operation Khukri:
Hostage Rescue in Sierra Leone

When over two hundred Indian soldiers on a United Nations peacekeeping mission in Sierra Leone were taken hostage by rebels, the international community looked the other way. The Nigerians seemed to derive pleasure from the Indians' misery, the Americans and British advocated 'patience and restraint' in the face of a volatile hostage crisis, and the UN was simply too effete to help. Ultimately, the Indians had no choice but to take matters into their own hands to extricate their soldiers from the dangerously trigger-happy rebels. And so Operation Khukri was launched, 10,000 kilometres away from India, in a steaming tropical forest in West Africa.

6.15 a.m., 15 July 2000, Kailahun, Sierra Leone, West Africa. A loud explosion shattered the early morning silence in this remote and backward eastern corner of the country covered with tropical equatorial forest, as six Indian para commandos detonated an explosive charge, breaching the wall of the military garrison. Through the breach came a convoy of Ashok Leyland military trucks and Mahindra jeeps, all painted white with 'UN' stenciled in blue on both sides. In the convoy were more than 200 soldiers of the Indian army's Gorkha battalion, trying to escape from the garrison at Kailahun. Rebels from the Revolutionary United Front (RUF), which had been waging civil war in Sierra Leone for close to a decade, had laid siege to the garrison for seventy-five days and, earlier that morning, Indian para commandos had landed in British Chinook helicopters to help the Gorkhas escape.

The trucks and jeeps of the convoy were being driven by Gorkha soldiers, infamous in the Indian army for their

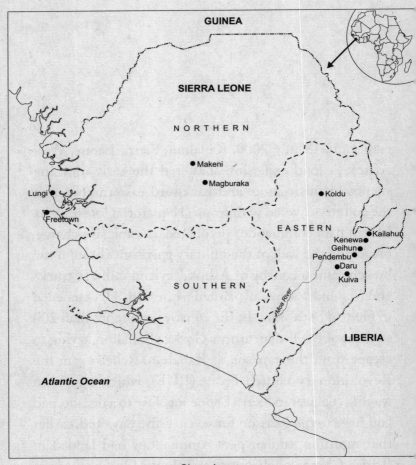

Sierra Leone

poor driving skills. But desperate times call for desperate measures. As the para commandos led the convoy out of the garrison, the vehicles got bogged down on the tracks, slushy after a heavy overnight downpour. The drivers pressed the accelerators, shifted to four-by-four gear drive, but still struggled to free the wheels from the marshy dirt tracks. There was no choice but for the soldiers to get down and push the trucks through the boggy areas. Meanwhile, they could hear the rebels gaining ground on them.

~

Indian soldiers had been deployed in Sierra Leone in 1999, as part of a UN peacekeeping mission, along with soldiers from more than a dozen other countries. Major General V.K. Jetley of the Indian army had been chosen to head the peacekeeping force in Sierra Leone, which had been torn apart by civil war since 1991. But shortly after the deployment, 223 Gorkha soldiers and eleven military observers of various nationalities were taken captive and held at the peacekeepers' Kailahun garrison by rebel forces. After diplomatic negotiations failed to secure their release, Jetley chose the military option. The helicopters in which the para commandos landed for the rescue operation were used to evacuate the military observers and a few ailing Gorkhas, while the rest of the Indian soldiers had to fight their way out in the trucks and jeeps stationed at their garrison.

By 7.50 a.m., the escape convoy had linked up with another team of para commandos at the Kailahun town centre. That team was led by Major Ajoy Mukherjee. The entire party was well secured, sandwiched between two groups of para commandos as they started their journey back to safety. Mukherjee was at the rear end of the column, guarding the most vulnerable point of the convoy.

But progress was slow because the vehicles frequently got bogged down in the slushy earth. The rebels, in the Toyota trucks that rebels around the world seem to favour, were in hot pursuit of the escaping Gorkhas and soon caught up with the column and started firing. Two para commandos were injured when a shoulder-fired rocket hit a tree, spraying them with splinters. Mukherjee ordered his men to trigger the booby traps and improvised explosive devices (IEDs) laid by them earlier that morning, to delay and deter the rebels. The para commandos simultaneously brought down heavy fire from medium machine guns and rocket launchers on to the rebels.

Mukherjee was particularly impressed with the damage caused by the airburst of the Karl Gustav 84mm rocket launcher. In an airburst, the rocket explodes in mid-air, above the target, instead of detonating after hitting it. With thick forest on both sides of the track, and the rebels at their heels, firing indiscriminately from their Toyota trucks, the Karl Gustavs came in handy. Mukherjee recounts, 'The airburst over the truck saw the rebels fall out of the vehicle like broken reeds in a storm.' For nearly forty-five minutes, the para commandos fought the rebels and tried to keep moving forward. They kept looking skyward for support, scouting for the Indian Air Force's Mi-35 attack helicopters up there.

Only Mukherjee had a radio set that could communicate with the IAF helicopters. The Indian helicopters, unlike the British Chinooks, had been delayed because they could not fly in bad weather. At around 9.30 a.m., the weather improved and the IAF pilot asked Mukherjee: *'Mukho, tu kahaan hai. Hum aa rahe hain.* [Where are you? We are coming.]' Mukherjee responded tetchily, *'Abhi tak kahaan thay?* [Where were you till now?]' The para commandos had been on the road for three hours, leading the Gurkha soldiers to safety while being fired on and chased by the rebels.

~

Situated by the Atlantic Ocean, and with Liberia and Guinea as its neighbours, Sierra Leone was a British colony till 1961. The West African country is mostly covered with thick tropical equatorial forest.

After eight years of civil war, in July 1999, all parties to the dispute – the democratically elected government, the Sierra Leonean army and the rebel group, the RUF – signed the Lomé Accord, under which they agreed to form a government of national unity.

In October 1999, the UN Security Council authorized the formation of the United Nations Mission in Sierra Leone (UNAMSIL) to help implement the Lomé Peace Accord. India agreed to contribute troops to UNAMSIL.

In November 1999, Major General V.K. Jetley was sent as UNAMSIL's military head, popularly called the Force Commander. Jetley, who later retired as a lieutenant general, had had a distinguished career in the Indian army and was selected after an interview process at the UN headquarters in New York. The choice of Force Commander for any UN peacekeeping mission is a critical one, and usually sees much hectic diplomatic negotiation in the UN Security Council. Jetley was among three shortlisted candidates – the other two were African military officers – called for an interview to New York. Three weeks later, he was told that he had been selected for the job.

Jetley comes from a family that boasts a long line of army officers, and he had commanded the prestigious

Siachen Brigade that defends India's interests in the disputed glacier – the highest battlefield in the world. Jetley had recently completed a stint as head of an infantry division when he was selected by the UN to start this new peacekeeping mission in Sierra Leone.

But the UNAMSIL under Jetley had a rather convoluted mandate. It was a Chapter Six peacekeeping mission – that is, it was mandated to settle disputes pacifically, through negotiation and mediation, not force. However, Jetley did have certain windows of opportunity to employ methods allowed to a Chapter Seven mission, including more forceful military intervention, if required.

Besides the Indian soldiers, Jetley had to take charge of Nigerians, Ghanaians, Guineans, Kenyans and, after the expansion of the mission in February 2000, Jordanians, Bangladeshis and yet more Indians. While Jetley headed the military component of the UN mission, the civilian side was headed by Oluyemi Adeniji, a Nigerian diplomat. Adeniji's official designation was Special Representative to the Secretary General in Sierra Leone, and Jetley was nominally supposed to report to him. Adeniji had, in fact, in typical UN fashion, been given the job as a compromise – because the Nigerians were annoyed at having been denied the position that Jetley had got. The Nigerians viewed Sierra Leone as a part of their sphere of influence and were unhappy to see an Indian

Force Commander in charge. Their annoyance and lack of support to Jetley would cause many problems in the mission. It didn't help matters that the Secretary General of the UN at that time was the Ghanaian Kofi Annan, and most diplomats from West African countries had a direct line to him. Jetley often received phone calls from Annan – highly unusual for a Force Commander – with the Secretary General getting into the nitty-gritty of the mission, no doubt a result of the frequent calls he received from the West Africans.

The actual deployment of military units into action was not the prerogative of the Force Commander. Which country's contingent would go where was decided by the UN Security Council. But even so, Jetley had to use all his persuasive powers, coercion and support from Indian military units to execute the Security Council's deployment orders for the African troops. The Ghanaians, for instance, were occupying the best hotel in the capital city of Freetown – in fact, the only functional hotel in the country – and were reluctant to move out of the lap of relative luxury to their deployment area in the centre of the country. They even violated Jetley's explicit written orders, and Jetley ultimately had to monitor their movements from a helicopter, while Indian military units provided transport assistance to the Ghanaians, for their deployment to central Sierra Leone to be executed.

The situation with the contingents from other countries was no better. They were unwilling to confront the rebels, and in one galling instance the Guinean army handed over their tanks and weapons to the rebels at the border of Guinea and Sierra Leone, when they were crossing over to join the mission! But, determined to make a success of a prestigious international assignment, Jetley kept up the pretence of cordiality with the other military contingents. In his heart, though, he had faith in the professional abilities of only the Indian military units in his mission.

~

By April 2000, the soldiers of the various countries that were part of the UNAMSIL had been deployed at the designated areas in Sierra Leone, and five 'Disarmament, Demobilization and Reintegration (DDR) camps' for RUF rebels had also been set up. Under the DDR process, rebels surrender to the UN peacekeepers, give up their weapons and are taught skills which allow them to be reintegrated as useful members of society. A sixth DDR camp was to come up in the diamond-rich areas of Koidu, a highly underdeveloped area where no government had ever managed to reach. But this area was also an RUF stronghold and, fearing a loss of control, the rebels were anxious about this move. They didn't want all their cadres to relinquish their weapons as this would dramatically reduce their bargaining power in the ongoing negotiations for future elections and government formation. In signing the Lomé Accord but not wanting to disarm, the RUF was no exception. Most rebel groups that have signed a UN-supervised peace agreement have refused to fully embrace the DDR process.

But in Sierra Leone, the situation came to a head on 1 May, when the RUF demanded that ten rebels who had surrendered at the DDR camp at Makeni be handed back. The Kenyans oversaw this camp, and they refused to hand over the men. Angered by the refusal, the RUF attacked the camp and simultaneously the Kenyan army's neighbouring positions at Makeni and Magburaka, and laid siege there, which resulted in a large number of Kenyan casualties. The rebels took as hostage 500 Kenyan UN peacekeepers and around a dozen military observers. UN military observers, though technically UN peacekeepers, are unarmed military officers from various countries who are supposed to observe and report on the situation without taking part in the hostilities.

The message to Jetley was plain. The RUF didn't care for the Lomé Peace Accord it had signed only months ago.

Like a good soldier, Jetley's first instinct was to launch

a military operation at Makeni and Magburaka to resolve the impasse. But Jetley was hamstrung by various international sensitivities while exploring the limited options for the use of force that were available to him. He ultimately planned a three-pronged offensive against the rebels. A company of Kenyan soldiers was to attack the RUF outside Makeni, while the Quick Reaction Company of the Indian army was moved in armoured personnel carriers to attack the rebels deployed around Magburaka. The aim of these two thrusts was to beat back the rebels laying siege to the Kenyan army's positions. Using these thrusts as anvil, the newly inducted Zambian battalion was to be put to work as hammer on the RUF. Unfortunately, while the Indians and Kenyans managed to fight their way into the former Kenyan positions at Makeni and Magburaka, the Zambian operation went awry. Half of the Zambians were tricked into captivity and taken hostage by the rebels. The UN military operation to rescue the Kenyan peacekeepers had failed, and miserably so.

~

To add insult to injury, the emboldened RUF rebels also surrounded Indian peacekeepers and eleven military observers from different countries at Kailahun,

400 kilometres east of the capital city of Freetown. They targeted the Kailahun garrison not for a military reason but because the UN peacekeepers' civic actions in that area had weakened the rebels' hold over the people. The RUF were desperate to regain their pre-eminence in the area.

In Kailahun, the government had been missing for a decade. It was not even connected by road with the rest of Sierra Leone. The Indian army's 5/8 Gorkha Rifles had been deployed by mid April 2000 deep inside the RUF-held territory at Daru, where the Gorkha battalion headquarters were established, and at Kailahun.

When Jetley first went there in March 2000, Kailahun was devoid of even a semblance of governance. There was a mass outbreak of disease, lack of food, no facilities for public health or education, and poverty was endemic. Jetley chose to win over the locals by bringing basic public amenities to the people through the Gorkha battalion. He got a military bridge made quickly – in just four days! – by Indian military engineers, opened UN medical camps, made provisions for clean drinking water and distributed food and medicines. He even flew people in need of urgent medical attention in UN helicopters to Freetown for treatment. The UN was adored by the locals.

Even the foot soldiers of the RUF siege at Kailahun

were apologetic about their action, and blamed it on their leadership. The rebels decided not to attack the Indian peacekeepers and were on friendly terms with them, so much so that on the basis of an honour code the rebels allowed the movement of food and medicine convoys from the battalion headquarters at Daru to the besieged Gorkhas at the Kailahun garrison.

But tensions escalated when the Gorkha battalion sent its second in command, with a patrol of twenty-two soldiers from Daru and their RUF liaison, to negotiate the release of the hostages at the Kailahun garrison. At Kuiva, 52 kilometres short of Kailahun, the patrol was stopped and surrounded by about 200 drugged-out rebels. The RUF rebels, many of them in their teens, were notorious for getting high on drugs and alcohol, and could be dangerously trigger-happy in that state. As the battalion had experienced similar situations many times before, the second in command tried to calm the rebels and began to negotiate with the local RUF commander, who told the patrol not to move forward under any circumstances as the situation was volatile and could spin out of hand.

The RUF leadership at Makeni had told its cadres that the UN had attacked them, which is why the patrol was detained. While the patrol was not ill-treated, and the

Indian soldiers were even permitted to arrange for food for themselves, they had, in effect, been captured.

Jetley was confronted with a serious situation. As on 2 May 2000, 223 Indian soldiers and eleven UN military observers were under siege at Kailahun, while twenty-three Indian soldiers were being held hostage at Kuiva. This was in addition to the failed military attack to rescue the 500 Kenyan peacekeepers in RUF captivity at Makeni and Magburaka.

~

Meanwhile, to get the Kenyan peacekeepers in RUF captivity released, the UN entered a protracted diplomatic negotiation with the rebels through the Liberian President, Charles Taylor. Taylor had a hold over the rebels and was considered the de facto leader of the RUF. He was later tried at the UN-backed Special Court for Sierra Leone at The Hague, and convicted in 2012 for supporting the RUF and giving them arms in exchange for 'blood diamonds'. Taylor was found guilty of aiding and abetting war crimes and crimes against humanity and unleashing a reign of terror through rape, sexual slavery, murder, public beheading and disembowelment, and forced amputation. But during the civil war, Taylor was a valuable conduit to the rebels for the international community. He was able to get the Kenyan hostages released but there was no progress on the Indian peacekeepers held captive at Kailahun and Kuiva. Some Indians felt that the Nigerians were playing dirty at that time, as a result of which Taylor was not willing to get the Indian peacekeepers released. Others believed that rebel organizations are not monolithic and Taylor, due to the limits of his influence with quasi-independent local rebel leaders, was helpless to do more.

Encouraged by the release of the Kenyan hostages, the Indian government too opened bilateral diplomatic negotiations with Taylor. A.K. Banerjee, India's high commissioner to Ghana at that time, started travelling to the Liberian capital, Monrovia, to negotiate with Taylor. While Taylor seemed keen to help, he stopped short of guaranteeing the release of the Indian soldiers. Banerjee felt that Taylor's influence didn't run deep enough with the local RUF commanders, but the Liberian President did not level with the Indians. During Banerjee's sixth visit to Liberia, Taylor's delegation made the usual, predictable request for aid from India, which Banerjee got sanctioned promptly.

As he was leaving after the meeting, Taylor walked out with Banerjee for a private chat. What the President said next caught the Indian diplomat by surprise.

'I have seen enough violence in my life and I don't want my children to be part of it. As a personal favour, could you help my two daughters secure admission in a college in India?' Taken aback but keen to do Taylor a favour which could in turn lead to the Indian soldiers being released, Banerjee pulled some strings at the foreign ministry in Delhi. Taylor's daughters were given admission in undergraduate courses at Lady Sriram College in Delhi.

Even so, the dreaded Liberian leader came through only partially for the Indians. The twenty-three Indian soldiers held captive at Kuiva were released thanks to Taylor's intervention and were flown to Freetown on 29 June 2000. But there was no breakthrough on the stand-off at Kailahun. The RUF rebels were desperate to hold on to the only bargaining chip they had for extracting concessions from the UN.

There was no solution in sight and Jetley was worried about the welfare of his men, especially about the impact on the morale of the Indian soldiers who had been surrounded by the rebels for such a long time. While the Gorkhas kept up their daily military routine at the Kailahun garrison, their spirits fell at the sight of the RUF rebels moving freely in their camp and picketing the fenced boundaries. The rebels were also mistreating the British military observer at the camp, dunking his head into a toilet and roughing him up. He had to pay the price for the anger against the British, the former colonial masters of Sierra Leone.

In early July 2000, RUF rebels abruptly stopped the supply of food to the Kailahun garrison, both by road and by air. They stopped allowing air evacuation of the sick and blocked the main road, running through the centre of the country, from Lungi to Freetown. Time was running out, and Jetley was nagged with worry about the loss of prestige for the Indian army. The diplomatic negotiations through the UN channels were still in full swing but going nowhere. In fact, it seemed that the Nigerians were happy at the discomfort of the Indians.

All this while, the British troops and helicopters present on Sierra Leonean soil neither became part of the UNAMSIL nor joined in any UN operation against the rebels. This is the peculiarity of most UN peacekeeping missions, which are decided on solely by the five permanent members of the UN Security Council. In most cases, the missions are in countries where one of the permanent members was the colonial ruler and is an interested party in the conflict. The permanent member that has an interest in that conflict-ridden country often stations its troops there – France in Cote d'Ivoire, for example – but never becomes part of the UN peacekeeping mission. This makes the job of the UN

Force Commander even more difficult, as Jetley found out in Sierra Leone.

In May 2000, before the Indian soldiers at Kuiva had been released, the UN Security Council agreed to increase the number of soldiers in the UNAMSIL to 13,000, including 260 military observers. Following this, two infantry battalions from Jordan and one battalion from Bangladesh came to Sierra Leone. India sent one more battalion, 18 Grenadiers, with one mechanized company, one engineer company and a flight of attack helicopters. By then, South Block was seriously considering a military solution for freeing the Indian soldiers and this was reflected in the composition of the Indian contingent. South Block would also send some elite para commandos to Sierra Leone.

~

A team of 135 para commandos, including five officers, of the 2 Para Special Forces battalion from Agra also became a part of the Indian contingent to Sierra Leone. The message from the army headquarters to officers of the 2 Para Special Forces battalion late in the evening of 10 May 2000 was rather cryptic: 'You are going for a special mission to a foreign country by the sea, full of thick forests and plagued by mosquitoes.'

Among those officers was Major Ajoy Mukherjee, who is now a colonel serving in Kashmir. Like everyone else, Mukherjee thought their destination was Sri Lanka. It ticked all the boxes – sea, forests, mosquitoes – and the Sri Lankan army had recently launched a fierce campaign against the Tamil Tigers.

They were, however, soon proved wrong when they learned that their destination was Sierra Leone, a country in West Africa none of them had the faintest idea of. They had been ordered to move to Delhi in double-quick time, from where they would be flown to Sierra Leone. Beyond that, the team knew nothing except that the Indian army had sent a contingent as part of the UN peacekeeping mission in the West African nation, and had got into some kind of trouble with the rebels.

In Delhi, the army headquarters briefed them about their task, and the formalities for foreign travel were completed at lightning speed. But the passports and visas of the 135 para commandos were not ready by the time they had to board a commercial flight for Freetown. As they boarded the Egyptian airlines plane, each para commando was given a stamped slip from the foreign ministry so that the immigration authorities in Sierra Leone would allow them to enter the country. As they were travelling on a commercial flight, the para commandos could carry only their personal weapons. All heavy weaponry was to follow later, on chartered flights.

But there were internal problems within the para commando team. The team commander, Major Harinder Sood, was not accepted by the other officers, as he had not gone through the full probation to become a para commando – the six-week period during which the physical and mental limits of every volunteer are tested before he is given the honour of wearing the Balidan (Sacrifice) badge on his left chest pocket. On top of that, the 135 para commandos were from various teams and had been put together hastily. They had neither operated nor trained as a single group before.

The para commandos landed at Freetown on 17 May and were based at Hastings airfield, a disused and dilapidated place. The next day they were assigned three tasks by Force Commander Jetley: one, rescue the twenty-three Indian soldiers held as hostages by the RUF at Kuiva (as mentioned earlier, these soldiers would be released only in June following Charles Taylor's negotiations); two, extricate the 223 Indian soldiers and eleven UN military observers from Kailahun; and last, recover the IAF's Mi-8 helicopter which had been forced to land in a field after it developed mechanical problems, some 150 kilometres inside rebel territory near Makeni.

While the para commandos were moved from India

most urgently, they weren't deployed immediately on a mission. The situation in Sierra Leone was quite complicated – many countries were involved; and besides, the UN diplomatic negotiations were proceeding via many channels and the hope was to get the soldiers released without initiating military action.

At Hastings airfield, the team from the 2 Para Special Forces battalion started training for the various plans to achieve its tasks. The para commandos started working with the British Special Air Service (SAS) team there. They were envious of the modern gadgetry, weaponry and equipment that the British commandos had. The good relations that the Indians commandos developed with the SAS men during their stay were to be of great help to Mukherjee and his men.

~

A daring plan to undertake a heliborne operation to rescue the twenty-three soldiers held at Kuiva had to be cancelled at the last minute, with Taylor's negotiations finally making headway and bearing fruit. The other task of recovering the helicopter from near Makeni also had to be shelved because it was assessed to be too risky. So only the task of rescuing the Indian soldiers and military observers at Kailahun remained.

More than two months had passed but there had been little progress. Senior Indian army officials including the Director General of Military Operations, Lt Gen. N.C. Vij, and his number two, Major General J.J. Singh – both of whom later became army chiefs – visited Sierra Leone to get a first-hand account of the ground situation. As all this was happening in the aftermath of the military victory at Kargil, there was little media coverage of the Kailahun siege in India. The reports from international media agencies were also sketchy. So there was no public uproar or outrage in India, a situation unimaginable in today's times.

Jetley had meanwhile been devising a military plan to extricate the hostages at Kailahun. A broad outline of a daylong plan was formulated. It was code-named Operation Khukri, after the slightly curved dagger traditionally carried by the Gorkhas.

But Jetley's plan still needed a couple of go-aheads. One of them was from New Delhi. Diplomatic efforts by the Indian government were not getting adequate response from London, New York or Washington, DC. Vij had travelled to these cities and got no assurance for help. He still sounds angry and bitter about the response from the US and UK governments. 'If only their soldiers had been part of those held captive, it would have been a different matter. We wouldn't have been lectured so much,' he said. The Americans and British paid lip service to the plight of the Indian soldiers but advocated discretion and restraint, and asked Vij to be patient. They were not willing to be party to any Indian decision to launch a military operation. By the end of the visit it was clear to him that 'no one was going to help us; we will have to do this on our own'.

Immediately on his return, Vij briefed the army chief, General V.P. Malik, who asked him to directly explain the situation to the defence minister, George Fernandes. Vij walked up to Fernandes's office in South Block and explained to him that, since all other options had been exhausted, a military operation in Sierra Leone was the only viable course of action left to free the Indian soldiers and UN military observers who had been in captivity for nearly two months now.

Fernandes was concerned about the potential number of Indian casualties if such action were launched. Vij assured him that it would be minimal but no one could guarantee that there would be no casualties at all. Within half an hour, Fernandes had been convinced, but he asked Vij to wait as he wanted the foreign minister, Jaswant Singh, to be briefed, too.

A former army officer, Jaswant Singh started by lecturing Vij on the geopolitical and geostrategic implications of military action in Sierra Leone. But Vij knew he would eventually come around to the army's point of view, as he always did. The former cavalryman just wanted to be certain that the army had weighed all its options carefully. The discussion lasted an hour, after which Jaswant Singh agreed, though reluctantly, that a military operation in Sierra Leone was the only choice left for the Indian army. The Indian soldiers at Kailahun might have been 'Blue Helmets' – that's what UN peacekeepers are popularly called – but they were still Indian soldiers.

After the foreign and defence ministers were brought on board, Prime Minister Atal Bihari Vajpayee was briefed about the plan. He concluded that it would be best to take into confidence the leaders of all political parties. An all-party meeting was held in South Block on an early July afternoon and was attended, among others, by Sonia Gandhi and Dr Manmohan Singh. Jaswant Singh explained the political aspects, while the military part of the briefing was given by Vij. Although no operational details were revealed, the broad contours of the military plan were shared with the political leaders.

The leaders repeatedly asked about the number of casualties expected in the operation. Vij was consistent: no guarantee could be given; casualties should be expected in any operation but they would be minimal considering the quality of training and equipment of the rebels. Vij said the army strongly felt that to preserve its honour as a professional institution, India had to take matters into its own hands. The time had come for the soldiers to be brought back and their humiliation put to an end. The hour-long discussion ended with all political parties unanimously endorsing the plan, which was to be executed a week later.

However, one question asked by Dr Manmohan Singh, then leader of the Opposition in the Rajya Sabha, was to have far-reaching consequences. 'Why are we there in Sierra Leone in the first place? What strategic interest of ours does it serve?' Vij had no answer but when he became army chief while Dr Singh was prime minister, the army started choosing UN assignments with greater care, refusing a few which would put Indian soldiers at great risk.

That was far in the future. At that point, 223 soldiers of 5/8 Gorkha Rifles were at great risk in Sierra Leone, in the midst of a chaotic and bloody conflict.

~

The second go-ahead that Jetley needed was from the UN. Jetley had been invited by Kofi Annan to an African Union meeting at Lomé, the capital of Togo. Annan took Jetley around and introduced him to the dignitaries.

When Jetley eventually got some time alone with the Secretary General, he broached the delicate issue for which he had flown down.

'Your Excellency, I need to undertake a military operation to retrieve the peacekeepers. I need your green signal for that,' Jetley said.

'The decision is yours, General,' was Annan's diplomatic reply, as he insisted that the operation had to include troops from countries other than India.

'Thank you, Your Excellency, I have got the answer,' was Jetley's reply. He walked away, knowing that if he made a hash of Operation Khukri, his head would be on the chopping block. But if he succeeded, Annan and everyone else would share in the glory. Confident about his plan, Jetley decided to go ahead with the operation.

~

The successful planning of Operation Khukri depended on good intelligence. The movement that was permitted to the twenty-three soldiers held at Kuiva – they were allowed, on an honour code basis, to go to Daru and Kailahun for medical relief and logistical supplies – had proved a godsend. This allowed Jetley to gain intelligence about RUF deployments on these critical routes and the weapons that the rebels had.

The rebels had initially also allowed the UN to evacuate casualties from Kailahun by air, which gave Jetley's men a bird's-eye view of the full rebel deployment. They took aerial pictures not only of the RUF deployments but also of open areas that could serve as landing zones for UN forces during operations. The broad details of the terrain and rebel deployment being available, the nuances were filled in a daring move by a young captain from 2 Para Special Forces.

Captain Dhiraj Thapa, a para commando officer, exploited his ethnic similarity with the Gorkha soldiers. The local RUF leader who was negotiating on behalf of the rebels had been given a UN vehicle and a Gorkha driver-cum-helper. On the pretext of being the Gorkha driver, Thapa managed to infiltrate the besieged Kailahun garrison, and blend in, armed with a digital camera and maps provided by the British SAS team.

For two weeks, he posed as the driver and general dogsbody of the RUF commander as he travelled between Kailahun and Daru, collecting vital target and terrain information all along. He sent back photographs of the location of the hostages, potential landing zones, rebel posts and other sites of military importance. It was a dangerous task, and eventually the RUF rebels figured out that there was a Special Forces operative collecting information about them. But before they could identify who he was, 2 Para Special Forces had pulled Thapa out.

By this time, Jetley had a clear picture of enemy deployment and the terrain. He knew that the rebels had their brigade headquarters at Pendembu, halfway between Daru and Kailahun. However, like any military commander, he felt that he could do with yet more intelligence. He tried hard to get a satellite image of the area but failed. With Thapa compromised and the rebels disallowing movement of Indian peacekeepers, no additional information was going to be available to Jetley. He had to make do with what he had.

Having been stung badly by the heavy politicking in the UN mission, where no one could be fully trusted, Jetley was paranoid about his operational plans being leaked. He had to go to extra lengths to keep them secret; he did not even share them with Adeniji or the other foreign contingents, despite their persistence. Jetley was particularly pressed by the British high commissioner to divulge the plans as one of their army officers was among the eleven military observers being held captive in Kailahun. As mentioned earlier, he was being mistreated by the rebels. Earlier, the British had tried to press Jetley for some ammunition from the Indian contingent, and he had refused. The matter had gone up to the Sierra Leonean President, but Jetley stood his ground. So his relationship with the British was not exactly friendly.

Despite the frosty relations, the British were desperate to know Jetley's plans so that they could find a way to extricate their man. Jetley also needed something from the British: their Chinook helicopters, as the Indian military helicopters, of Soviet origin, were not capable of flying at night or in bad weather. Finally, an agreement was reached that suited both parties. Jetley would integrate some SAS operatives as part of the mission, and in return the British army would provide two Chinook helicopters for the operation. Operation Khukri was now all set to be launched.

~

Jetley estimated the RUF had a strength of 1700–1800 rebels in the area. Most of them were poorly trained and had only small arms. They had no artillery guns, tanks or air support available to them. On his side, Jetley had two Indian infantry battalions (5/8 Gurkha Rifles and 18 Grenadiers), two companies each of Nigerian and Ghanaian troops, one Quick Reaction Company, one mechanized infantry company, one composite artillery battery, one engineer company, a mobile surgical unit and an Indian aviation unit. In addition, he had the team of 2 Para Special Forces.

The total count of his fighting troops came to 1963 soldiers, and he had another 308 supporting troops in his contingent: a combat ratio of roughly 1:1 with the RUF rebels in the theatre of operation, whereas according to conventional wisdom this should be 3:1 for the attacker to succeed. But Jetley had a definite edge over the rebels. His men had attack helicopters, transport helicopters, artillery and mechanized infantry, and special forces. The British contribution of two Chinook helicopters and one C-130 Hercules aircraft to block the rebels' wireless radio communications also acted as force multipliers. Additional UN helicopter flights of Mi-8, Mi-17 and Mi-26 helicopters were also chartered by Jetley.

As Jetley repeatedly emphasizes, the operation was 'multinational, multidimensional and multidirectional'.

On D-day, that is, 15 July 2000, the original plan was to start with a pre-emptive strike by British helicopters at Pendembu, the rebels' brigade headquarters, and Kailahun. But the British refused, saying that Operation Khukri's element of surprise would be lost, and so the plan was modified to have the 2 Para Special Forces assault team land at Kenewa, near Kailahun, to take control of the Kenewa–Kailahun route, which was to be used later by the Gorkhas to escape. They were to land using British Chinook helicopters, which would then go on to Kailahun, with Thapa, and five other para commandos, on board as he knew the place first-hand, and pick up the unarmed military observers, wounded and sick Indian soldiers, and warlike stores. The rest of the Gorkha battalion troops at Kailahun would escape southward towards Daru, with the assistance of Thapa and his team – this would entail stiff fighting for 70 kilometres en route, through the heartland of RUF territory.

After they had taken control of Kenewa, the assault team of 2 Para Special Forces was tasked to meet the Gorkhas at the Kailahun town centre to help them fight their way back to Daru. The operation was expected to last for thirty hours.

But operations rarely go as planned and Operation Khukri was no exception. On the night of 14 July, the weather turned bad, with low clouds and heavy rains. The para commandos reached the airfield at 3 a.m. on 15 July and boarded the two Chinook helicopters. The C-130 Hercules aircraft took off at 4 a.m. to start jamming the rebels' wireless radio communication. The downpour was so heavy that Mukherjee asked the SAS if the helicopters would take off at all. He was somewhat surprised when the SAS guy replied in the affirmative. The two helicopters took off by 5.20 a.m. and Mukherjee remembers the flight distinctly as it followed the course of the River Moa, with the second helicopter visible on the horizon. 'It was a scene straight out of a Hollywood movie,' he says.

Mukherjee and his men had practised with the SAS and Chinooks for two days. The Indian para commandos were used to slithering down from helicopters by slow roping – using soft gloves to move down the two sets of mountaineer's climbing rope twined together. When they tried the soft gloves with the thick ropes dangling from the Chinook for the first time during practice, Mukherjee came down so quickly that he had to use his legs to catch hold of the rope and slow his fall. Two of his men on the adjacent ropes were not so lucky. One of them broke his back and the other his knee as they landed with a thud on the tarmac. The para commandos then altered their drill. They started using their feet to slow down their slithering.

The leading Chinook was nearing the destination and the SAS sergeant gave the 'five minutes to go' warning. Mukherjee saw the chopper pressing down into the forest with full force and by the time they were at the target the helicopter was inside the trees, pressing downwards as the trees bent and broke under the pressure.

In the deafening din, the SAS sergeant put his hand in front of Mukherjee and gestured with his fingers: five, four, three, two, one. Mukherjee was the first to slither down and although he had told his men to wait till he gave them the go-ahead, in the excitement of the moment, no one waited. They slithered down immediately after him. Mukherjee looked at the GPS. Forty of his men had landed at the exact spot that was decided, near the track junction at Kenewa. He deployed his men to lay booby traps and IEDs, as the Chinook lifted off towards Kailahun, with Thapa and five other para commandos on board.

The sound of the Chinooks had warned the RUF rebels at Kailahun but they were sluggish in the morning. Thapa landed at Kailahun where the military observers and Indian peacekeepers were already waiting for him – they had been told over the radio the evening before that they should be ready to move, and that no important military equipment should be left behind. Thapa and his men dealt with the rebels effectively by bringing down a heavy volume of fire on them, and liberally using the phosphorous grenades supplied to them by the SAS. The military observers and some unwell Indian peacekeepers managed to board the Chinook, which then took off towards safety. With the British peacekeeper safely on the Chinook, the Indians knew that the British wouldn't allow them to use their helicopters any more.

By 6.15 a.m., the beleaguered Gorkha troops had successfully broken out of the camp in jeeps and trucks through the breach in the wall made by Thapa and his men. They met Mukherjee's men at the Kailahun town centre by 8 a.m. The entire party of over 200 men who had been under siege for seventy-five days was well secured between two groups of para commandos as they started their journey back. As mentioned earlier, Mukherjee was the rearguard of the column, from where the rebels were most likely to attack.

The movement of the column was slow because of the poor state of the track and the vehicles were frequently getting stuck in the slushy mud. Ultimately, the rebels caught up with the escaping convoy from behind and started firing. After defending themselves against persistent RUF fire for forty-five minutes, the Indian soldiers were finally able to establish contact with the IAF attack helicopters that had been unable to fly due to the bad weather till then. The skies had cleared up, and the IAF pilot asked Mukherjee, the only one in the convoy with a radio set, to indicate the area beyond which it was safe for them to strafe. The SAS had lent the para commandos some coloured phosphorous grenades and Mukherjee threw the first one that came to his hand. It was an orange smoke grenade. 'Everything north of the orange smoke is the enemy. Do as you deem fit with them,' he told the pilot.

The attack helicopters started strafing with rockets and

guns, clearing two kilometres of road immediately, and kept up the pounding for over two hours. As the attack helicopters had limited endurance, they relieved each other in rotation to sustain the barrage. The Indians had lent 700 rockets to the two attack helicopters of the Sierra Leonean army, which were operated by South African mercenaries. It was a free-for-all after that.

Jetley was in the air in a Cheetah helicopter as the 200-odd Gorkha soldiers, protected by the para commandos, linked up with the column of 18 Grenadiers at Geihun at 10.30 a.m. He landed there to greet them. Geihun had been captured by the Grenadiers at 8 a.m. in a heliborne operation. Sixty-five Gorkha soldiers were heli-lifted from there, while the rest moved on road to link up with Indian soldiers at Pendembu.

But this link-up was delayed as the rebels had dug up the road between Geihun and Pendembu, and deployed themselves in the thickly wooded area along those road blocks. Jetley ordered the Indian sapper company to move flexible duckboards to repair the cratered roads, which allowed the Gorkha soldiers to continue moving in their vehicles, as Mukherjee guarded the rear of the convoy. Jetley was surprised at the radio communication network of the rebels, which allowed them to move their men quickly. The overwhelming firepower of the UN forces, both on the ground and the air, was, however, too much for the RUF to counter.

Pendembu had to be captured by 5/8 Gorkha Rifles, to allow the Kailahun column to be heli-lifted from there. But the RUF put up strong opposition to the Gorkhas and Pendembu's capture was delayed till 7 p.m. All the columns were forced to stay at Pendembu for the night, where they came under heavy fire from the rebels. Twice the scout helicopter observed regrouping RUF rebels approaching Pendembu and it directed the Mi-35 attack helicopters to carry out dissuading strikes on them using rockets and guns. Approach paths to the town were also shelled by mortars and a 105mm light field gun throughout the night, to repel rebel assaults.

The next day the beleaguered Gorkhas who had spent seventy-five days under siege were heli-lifted to Daru, from where the para commandos were sent to Freetown. The Indians suffered their only fatal casualty that afternoon after the main operation when a vehicle was hit by a rebel RPG rocket in a different area. Besides that fatality, only seven Indians were injured in the operation. In contrast, thirty-four rebels had been killed and another 150 wounded by the UN peacekeepers in a single day, breaking the back of the RUF. A large number of weapons, including a surface-to-air missile, four rocket-propelled grenades, twelve AK-47s, six general purpose machine guns, three heavy machine guns and anti-personnel mines, were captured from the rebels, denuding their fighting capacity for the future. However, of even greater importance was the message sent to Sierra Leoneans at large that the UN forces could strike the RUF in their heartland – which completely demoralized the rebels.

~

Their job done, the para commandos from 2 Para Special Forces returned to India, after spending four months in the faraway African country. Operation Khukri had established the professional competence of the Indian army and Indian air force in an international setting. Peace in the strife-torn country was still a few years away but it broke the myth of RUF supremacy and brought the rebels to the negotiating table.

George Fernandes flew to Freetown to felicitate the Indian soldiers who had participated in the operations. Accolades for the successful military operation poured in from all over the globe, including a letter from Kofi Annan to Jetley, on 17 July 2000, which stated:

I should like to extend to you my gratitude and admiration for the thoroughly professional manner in which you, your military staff and the troops on the ground have planned and executed the extraction of the surrounded peacekeepers at Kailahun. The fact that there were only a few casualties on our side is a clear indication of the determination of the force, as well as of its robustness in dealing with any threats from the RUF.

But the best tribute came from the people of Sierra Leone, who helped build the Khukri War Memorial on the bank of the River Moa. That was a well-earned reward for a bold operation launched by Indian soldiers 10,000 kilometres away from home.

Acknowledgements

'You never know what you are going to write until you start writing.' Whoever said that got it absolutely right. As with all books, the writing of *Mission Overseas* started with a good dose of enthusiasm, but I was able to complete it thanks to a combination of love, luck and labour.

This book's genesis lies in my conversations with former-armyman-turned-historian Srinath Raghavan, who was instrumental in pushing me to take up the challenge. Not only did he recommend my name to publishers, without ever letting me know, he was always forthcoming with all possible help, with his encouragement, insights and research, during the writing of this book.

Ronen Sen, A.K. Banerjee, Gen. N.C. Vij, Lt Gen. Vinod Bhatia, Lt Gen. V.K. Jetley, Maj. Gen. Sheonan Singh, Maj. Gen. Dalbir Singh, Group Capt. A.K.

Chordia, Col Ranbir Bhadauria, Col Ajoy Mukherjee and many others who asked not to be named were generous with their time and information while sharing detailed personal accounts of the operations. Special thanks are also due to those who shared old documents and unreleased official papers about these operations, which helped me get a better picture of these missions overseas.

This is also my chance to respond to my friends – Sarah Farooqui, Ankur Bhardwaj, Seema Chishti, Mihir Sharma, Aruna Urs, Sachin Kalbag, Nitin Pai and Smita Prakash – who have pestered me incessantly about writing a book, while supplying me with ideas, suggestions, feedback and a lot of reassurance. I hope they will stay quiet for some time now.

This book would not have been possible without the two organizations that I have loved working with: the Indian Army, for two decades, and the *Indian Express*, for far less time. Each of my colleagues at the two institutions has enriched me deeply, which I hope is reflected in this book in some manner. At the *Indian Express*, my thanks to Raj Kamal Jha and Unni Rajen Shanker for making it possible.

To my publisher, Chiki Sarkar, and editors, Nandini Mehta and Parth Mehrotra, I couldn't have asked for a more professional set of people to work with. It is an association I cherish and value.

Acknowledgements

To my parents and my brother, Prashant, I hope this effort redeems me somewhat for all the liberties I have taken over the years as the youngest of the family.

Above all, to my infinitely better half, Sakshi, without whom, not only this book but most other things in life would have remained incomplete.

A Note on the Author

Sushant Singh is Associate Editor with the *Indian Express*. He served for two decades with the Indian army, including several stints in Jammu and Kashmir and as a military observer with the United Nations.

THE APP
FOR INDIAN
READERS

Fresh, original books tailored for mobile and for India. Starting at ₹10.

juggernaut.in

1

CRAFTED
FOR MOBILE
READING

*Thought you would never read a book
on mobile? Let us prove you wrong.*

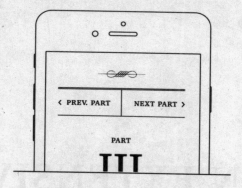

Beautiful Typography

The quality of print transferred
to your mobile. Forget ugly PDFs.

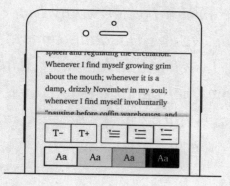

Customizable Reading

Read in the font size, spacing
and background of your liking.

2

AN EXTENSIVE LIBRARY

Including fresh, new, original Juggernaut books from the likes of Sunny Leone, Praveen Swami, Husain Haqqani, Umera Ahmed, Rujuta Diwekar and lots more. Plus, books from partner publishers and loads of free classics. Whichever genre you like, there's a book waiting for you.

3

DON'T JUST READ; INTERACT

We're changing the reading experience from passive to active.

Ask authors questions

Get all your answers from the horse's mouth.
Juggernaut authors actually reply to every
question they can.

Rate and review

Let everyone know of your favourite reads or
critique the finer points of a book – you will be
heard in a community of like-minded readers.

Gift books to friends

For a book-lover, there's no nicer gift than
a book personally picked. You can even
do it anonymously if you like.

Enjoy new book formats

Discover serials released in parts over
time, picture books including comics,
and story-bundles at discounted rates.
And coming soon, audiobooks.

4

LOWEST PRICES & ONE-TAP BUYING

Books start at ₹10 with regular discounts and free previews.

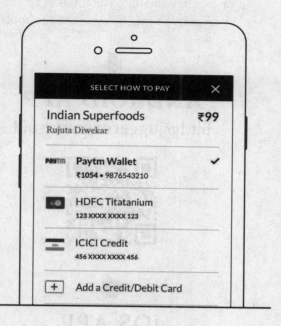

Paytm Wallet, Cards
& Apple Payments

On Android, just add a Paytm Wallet once and
buy any book with one tap. On iOS, pay with one
tap with your iTunes-linked debit/credit card.

Click the QR Code with a QR scanner app
or type the link into the Internet browser
on your phone to download the app.

ANDROID APP

bit.ly/juggernautandroid

iOS APP

bit.ly/juggernautios

For our complete catalogue, visit www.juggernaut.in
To submit your book, send a synopsis and two
sample chapters to books@juggernaut.in
For all other queries, write to contact@juggernaut.in